Dimensions of *Musical* Thinking

Dimensions of *Musical* Thinking

Edited by
Eunice Boardman

MUSIC EDUCATORS NATIONAL CONFERENCE

Acknowledgments

The Authors

Hilary Apfelstadt is an associate professor of music education at the University of North Carolina, Greensboro.

Barbara Alvarez is an assistant professor of music education at Ball State University, Muncie, Indiana.

Janet R. Barrett is a lecturer in the School of Music, University of Wisconsin-Madison.

Eunice Boardman, Editor, is a professor of music and education and is the Director of the School of Music at the University of Wisconsin-Madison.

Mark DeTurk is an assistant professor of music education at the University of New Hampshire, Durham.

Richard Kennell is an assistant professor of performance studies at Bowling Green State University, Bowling Green, Ohio.

Brian Moore is an assistant professor of music education at the University of Nebraska-Lincoln.

Mary P. Pautz is an assistant professor of music education at the University of Wisconsin-Milwaukee.

Lenore Pogonowski is an associate professor of music education at Teachers College, Columbia University, New York.

Betty Welsbacher is a professor of music education at Wichita State University, Wichita, Kansas.

ISBN 0-940796-62-7

Table of Contents

Foreword

Thinking as the Foundation of Music Learning

Who would not agree that helping students learn to think, to use information in intelligent ways, has always been an important goal of schooling? Yet many of the documents that appeared in the early 1980s spoke strongly to the perception that our young people were coming out of school ill-prepared to function in the information society of the latter part of this century, particularly in the application of higher order thinking skills to the solving of complex problems.

In response to this oft-stated concern, in 1985 twenty-four organizations, including the Music Educators National Conference, formed the Association Collaborative on Teaching Thinking. One of the most important results of this collaborative to date is the publication of *Dimensions of Thinking: A Framework for Curriculum and Instruction* (Marzano et al. 1988). While there was no intent by the authors of this book to provide a "definitive" scope and sequence for the teaching of thinking, it does provide a cohesive framework on which individuals or groups may begin to build their own structure applicable to their subject field. In the first chapter, "Thinking as the Foundation of Schooling," the authors identify the goal of education to be the development "of mature thinkers who are able to acquire and use knowledge" (Marzano et al. 1988, 2). Recognizing this as the ultimate goal, the need for a framework for teaching thinking, or teaching students to think, becomes urgent. To provide a framework for thinking about teaching thinking, five dimensions are specified: metacognition, critical and creative thinking, thinking processes, core thinking skills, and the relationship of content-area knowledge to thinking.

This volume, *Dimensions of Musical Thinking*, focuses on the fifth dimension, the relationship of content-area knowledge to thinking, and seeks to demonstrate ways that teachers can structure classroom environments where students not only learn specific musical content and skills but also "learn how to learn" to think musically.

Each of the chapters of *Dimensions of Musical Thinking* incorporates the major points found in *Dimensions of Thinking*[1] into a discussion of ways music teachers may ensure that their students become independent musical thinkers by applying appropriate thinking processes to the achievement of musical goals.

Eunice Boardman

---

1. As this book, *Dimensions of Thinking: A Framework for Curriculum and Instruction*, published by the Association for Supervision and Curriculum Development, will be referred to frequently throughout this volume, it will not be referenced in subsequent chapters unless there is a citation from a specific page. The book is available from MENC Publication Sales.

1

THE RELATION OF MUSIC STUDY TO THINKING

EUNICE BOARDMAN

In chapter 5 of *Dimensions of Thinking*, titled "The Relationship of Content-Area Knowledge to Thinking," the authors present the views of those who aver that thinking skills must be taught within a meaningful (that is, specific subject matter) context. This rationale is based on recognition that two pitfalls await us at either extreme. If the focus is on acquisition of knowledge "for knowledge's sake," the result may easily be meaningless rote learning that has no possibility of transfer. However, learning thinking skills "in a vacuum" is equally meaningless. One must think about something! Thus the emphasis in this chapter is one of relating the development of thinking processes to the acquisition of a particular body of content. Within the chapter four perspectives on content knowledge and the implications of various thinking dimensions on each are presented. These perspectives are: content-area learning as schema-depen-

1

dent, content areas as models and metaphors, content areas as changing bodies of knowledge, and content areas as special approaches to investigation.

To help students become independent musicians to the extent of their interest and ability is an unverbalized, if not actually stated, goal of every music educator. In pursuit of this goal in the 1960s, members of the profession sought to identify what was to be taught, to define the content that forms the knowledge domain known as music.

Today that content has become fairly well defined, at least in general music programs (both elementary and secondary), as consisting of concepts related to the elements of music and how these elements interact within a musical whole. Along with the definition of content came a similar endeavor to clarify how students exhibit their understanding of music. This "how" was translated into a definition of musical behaviors to include performing, describing, and creating. With the "what" and the "how" clearly specified, the profession seemed to feel that the curricular structure in relation to the goals of music education was well established and problems of achievement had been solved.

However, as we moved into the 1980s, music educators, as well as other teachers, recognized that specifying content and behavior was not enough—that somehow the students who were leaving our music programs were no better prepared to interact with music independently than were those who had participated in school music programs of the fifties and sixties. Something was still missing. Drawing on propositions made by researchers and practitioners in the general field of education and educational psychology, we have gradually come to realize that, unless we help students develop appropriate thinking processes—that is, learn how to think about music, how to draw on existing musical information and skill (content and behavior) in order to learn to perform a new piece of music, and how to respond to an unfamiliar composition or to express one's own musical ideas through improvisation and composition—the time spent in the music classroom has been essentially wasted. How to help students learn appropriate cognitive skills and the understanding of how to use those skills to gain knowledge and musical skill must be the focus of each teacher's planning if the goal stated earlier in this chapter—to help students become musically independent—is to be attained.

Content Areas as Special Approaches to Investigation

The final perspective on the relation of content to thinking offered in *Dimensions of Thinking* may well be the most significant for those of us teaching music. In discussing this theme, authors propose that each domain has special ways of thinking typically used by specialists in that field. Too often, subject study does not provide for engaging in thinking as searching for ways to solve real problems. Students read "about" history, rather than engaging in the historian's methods of investigation to solve a problem of import to them. They "pretend" to engage in tasks requiring mathematical skills, such as running a grocery store or completing a tax form. While setting up a model student government may be a better way to help students understand the processes involved in effective legislative practices than simply reading about the form of government of the United States, it still is not reality and the students know it.

In contrast, students involved in performance, description, or creation of music are engaging in the same kinds of thinking as the professional, albeit at a simpler level. Because of the potential for meaningful learning within the music classroom, music teachers can have a great advantage over other teachers in helping students learn music, provided that the primary focus within the music class is on learning music and musicianly behaviors rather than learning "about" things peripheral to music (for example, the label "quarter note" for a particular squiggle, the date of Bach's birth). Students will be motivated to learn, will come to the class ready to attend, committed to following through on the task at hand, whether it be expanding one's ability to understand the written score in order to become a more proficient performer; extending one's knowledge of structure by analyzing contrasting segments within a symphonic work so as to become a more discriminating describer; or exploring parameters of timbre while improvising, thus becoming a more sensitive creator of music.

Content-Area Learning as Schema-Dependent

A considerable body of research exists that suggests that information is organized in the memory in "packages" known as *schemata* (Neisser 1976). A schema enables the individual to make links between previous and present activities, to have expectations about what will occur and thereby to be able to act appropriately (Mandler 1985). In music one may have a schema for concert attendance, for approaching the study of a new piece of music, or for composing a melody based on a particular tonal organization. In each case, one possesses knowledge of the sequence of activities to be undertaken, the appropriate behavior needed for each segment within the activity, and the knowledge needed to execute that behavior. Obviously such a complex network of knowledge and action does not occur without many repetitions and adjustments, as needed, to take new information into account.

There are a number of implications of schema theory that we as teachers can use in helping students become skilled music learners. First, schema are

3

expanded and refined through the assimilation of new information into existing structures. For example, young children may possess an adequate schema for learning to sing a new piece of music that involves listening to the teacher, focusing on various aspects of the sound in response to the teacher's instructions, and eventually repeating the complete song. As students are introduced to the idea that one can learn to sing a new song by following notation, the existing schema must be expanded and refined. To assure that this adjustment occurs, the teacher must help the learner associate the new (that is, determining melodic rhythm by following notation) with the familiar (determining melodic rhythm by following iconic representations or through listening for longer and shorter sounds).

Another advantage of the use of schemata is the ability to infer, to predict. Attending a concert and noting that Mozart is on the program enables the possessor of the appropriate *content schemata* (in this case, the content being stylistic characteristics typical of Mozart's time) to make predictions about what will be heard, to use that information to enjoy listening to the music, even if it is a Mozart concerto never before heard. It is the task of the teacher to set up experiences that make it possible for the learner to gain the appropriate knowledge and skill necessary for this scenario.

Schemata theory recognizes that knowledge exists as a network of interrelated pieces of information that enable the learner to act appropriately in new situations; schemata theory makes the concept of transfer possible—to demonstrate that learning can truly be generative in the sense that what is learned in one situation enables the learner to solve the next musical problem more efficiently. One task of the music teacher is to identify the schemata that guide musicianly behavior and to base music instruction on helping students internalize them to the extent that the students can function as independent musicians. The acquisition of such schemata at some level of complexity should be the goal of the music teacher, whether working with a first-grade general music class or a high school orchestra.

Content Areas as Models and Metaphors

Schwartz and Ogilvy (1979) suggest that subject areas should be thought of as models or metaphors for reality. Models and metaphors provide a mental map of the actual world, with each map (or subject matter) offering a different understanding of the nature of things. Certainly those of us in music education have long known that the value of music, its very existence as an art form, lies in the fact that it provides a representation of the world that is unique. Langer (1948) may have stated it most clearly when she identified music as symbol, as representing the "form of feeling."

There is no question that those who best understand any field of human knowledge do so because they have grasped the essential nature of that field as a model of reality. As music teachers, it is crucial that we not lose sight, in our anxiety over the next concert or tuning the autoharps, of our ultimate mission—to help our students grasp the deeper meaning of musical structure and thus gain the ability to use music as a metaphor of reality. Drilling rhythm patterns, recalling tonal syllables, practicing the correct fingering ad infinitum may be necessary activities at some point, but only if the learner sees how the focus on the part leads to a more complete sensitivity to the whole. This cannot occur unless the teacher regularly helps the student make that connection.

Content Areas as Changing Bodies of Knowledge

In the opening chapter of *Dimensions of Thinking* the authors briefly summarize the chronology of the changing views of the human mind offered by psychologists and philosophers since the mid-nineteenth century. They point out that much of the current emphasis on skill practice stems from the principles proffered by the behavioral psychologists, including E. L. Thorndike, C. L. Hull, C. E. Osgood and B.F. Skinner. More recently, cognitive psychologists have proposed theories that are a major source of influence for the principles presented in this book. Some of the changes that have occurred as a result of cognitive theories are reflected in our changing definition of knowledge as well as changes in our assumptions about how knowledge is acquired and the interaction between knowledge and behavior. Music psychologists have also increasingly turned to the role of cognition as it influences our perceptions of music. (See, for example, Dowling and Harwood 1986; Howell, Cross, and West 1985; and Sloboda 1985.) The implications of some of the research conclusions for teachers concerned with helping students become thinking musicians will be presented in the following chapters.

Dimensions of Musical *Thinking* is organized into two parts. The first part parallels the organization of its companion volume, *Dimensions of Thinking: A Framework for Curriculum and Instruction.* Four chapters provide insights into the primary dimensions of thinking, as defined by the authors of *Dimensions of Thinking,* with emphasis on the implications of these dimensions for teaching and learning music. Part two turns to the particular problems of various specialty areas within the broad field of music education. Separate chapters on general music, the choral and instrumental rehearsal, music for the young child, the special learner, and the future teacher focus on ways teachers can ensure that their students are learning to think musically. The book ends

5

with a brief discussion of the implications of technology for musical thinking.

While each author was assigned a specific task, and speaks to the topic from a particular viewpoint, some common threads emerge that suggest the dawning of a new era in professional music education as significant as that which occurred in the sixties. The authors represented in this book come from many parts of the country and represent diverse interests within music education, yet they reveal a commonality of purpose and focus that defines both reaffirmation of previous goals and the establishment of new directions. The first of these is the constant reiteration of the recognition that the primary goal of *every* music educator, regardless of specialty, is to help students gain musical independence in order to engage in life-long musical learning once formal education is over. While this has been spoken to in the past, the difference found in this volume lies in the next commonality: the recognition that the music learning environment must include provision of opportunities for students to be involved in all three basic musical behaviors—performing, describing, and creating. The importance of such a broad experience is stressed as strongly by the authors of the chapters on musical thinking in the choral and instrumental rehearsals as it is by the author of the chapter on general music where this broad emphasis has existed for thirty years. Implicit in this second area of agreement is a third, which is sometimes verbalized but always present—the acknowledgment of the *reality* of music.

Music as a subject within the schools possesses a characteristic that makes it almost unique among the traditional school curricula: Musical experiences are (or have the potential of being) the same as—not pale imitations of—"real" music experiences in "real" life. Because of this reality, students, given the freedom and the challenge, will indeed "think musically," for they intuit the value of the learning event. Finally, all authors agree, as the circle is made complete, that the key to musical independence lies in metacognition—in learning how to monitor one's own thinking, to maintain executive control.

As you read this volume, the authors encourage you to personally employ the dimensions of thinking. As you progress through the book, metacognitively monitor your thinking as you compare the environment for thinking described in the various chapters with the thinking environment found within your own classroom. You may wish to begin by critically evaluating the themes, previously summarized, in relation to the goals and objectives of your own music teaching, and then consider the ideas presented in subsequent chapters as to how they may be incorporated into your own teaching so that your students also may: become musically independent; have opportunities to engage in performing, describing and creating; recognize that music, and musical experiences, are a metaphor of reality; and engage in metacognition as their personal key to musical independence.

2

METACOGNITION: A DIMENSION OF MUSICAL THINKING

LENORE POGONOWSKI

This chapter explores implications for music education of selected research and chapter 2 of *Dimensions of Thinking* on the subject of "metacognition."

Metacognition in the study of music involves skills associated with individual awareness and personal thinking. Students begin to see themselves as designers of their own learning rather than viewing musical information as something to be gleaned strictly from a teacher or a textbook.

If, for example, I notice that I am having more trouble executing a mordent than a trill or if it strikes me to look at the final cadence in a section of music before deciding to analyze a part of it in a certain key, I am exercising metacognitive thinking skills. If, as a fifth grader, I am aware that the ostinato I created is more interesting when each pitch has a unique dynamic level or as an eighth grader it occurs to me to try an alternate fingering in a difficult passage, I am extending my metacogntive thinking skill.

One of the most salient characteristics of metacognition is that it involves growing consciousness. Individuals become more aware of their thinking processes and more conscious of themselves as thinkers and performers (Presseisen 1985, 46).

According to Brown (1978) and the authors of *Dimensions of Thinking* the developmental psychologist John Flavell has been primarily responsible for the current interest in research in this area. As Flavell (1976, 232) describes:

> "Metacognition" refers to one's knowledge concerning one's own cognitive processes and products or anything related to them, e.g., the learning-relevant For example, I am engaging in metacognition...if I notice that I am having more trouble learning A than B, if it strikes me that I should double-check C before accepting it as a fact; if it occurs to me that I had better scrutinize each and every alternative in any multiple-choice type task situation before deciding which is the best one; if I sense that I had better make a note of D because I may forget it.... Metacognition refers, among other things, to the active monitoring and consequent regulation and orchestration of these processes in relation to the cognitive objects on which they bear, usually in the service of some concrete goal or objective.

We can determine that students are becoming more aware of their own thinking as they learn to describe what goes on in their heads when they think (Costa 1985, 189). In music classes this growing consciousness can be observed When students interact in small and large group improvisational settings where their choices about the uses of the parameters of music become more selective over time. As participants in discussions about music, students reveal their growing consciousness by the way they reflect about the music they create, perform or hear.

A metacognitive analogy to practicing the piano would be that, by being aware of how I want a particular phrase of music to sound, I have more control over getting it to sound that way. Using the same analogy but without metacognitive thinking, we can recall an experience from our formative years. As we practiced to memorize an "Allemande" from a *French Suite* by J. S. Bach, we found our thoughts elsewhere than with the music when we arrived at the end of the movement. While our fingers definitely had a workout, our metacognitive processes were not monitoring or controlling the quality of the product. A good performance, therefore, would be a matter of chance without the active regulation of metacognitive thinking skills.

Creating, listening, and performing are musical behaviors upon which activities basic to most music education curriculums are developed. Students can become aware of their potential for metacognitive thinking within the framework of each of these behaviors if the teacher plans appropriate strategies to encourage it. One example includes the use of a tape recorder for recording and playback, especially during performing and creating activities.

Performing

It is possible for students to sit through an entire rehearsal and only be aware of their own parts. In a performance setting in general music class, or in chorus, orchestra, and band rehearsals, students can learn to think more effectively about and beyond their particular parts. With the use of a tape recorder, music teachers can provide students with an opportunity to reflect on the effectiveness of their own performances. This can be handled by tape recording a piece as it is rehearsed and then listening to that tape and sharing suggestions for improvement. The music teachers could focus these suggestions by asking the students to evaluate what they did, how well they did it, what worked well and what did not, and what they would do differently next time. Suggestions from the students for improved performance could then be implemented during the rehearsal.

As we think about helping students develop metacognitive thinking in the rehearsal and performance setting, "The crucial task is to make it possible for them (the students) to learn to set goals and identify strategies for themselves" (Barell, Liebmann, and Sigel 1988, 17). These goals and strategies, along with those of the teacher, will help bring to the foreground individual metacognitive thinking and what we might consider as collective metacognitive thinking.

Collective metacognitive thinking may be brought about as a consequence of shared views. An example of this can be seen in the way we may be affected as mature musicians in our own interpretation of a given musical work by listening to a variety of artists' renditions of the same work. In a sense, by considering alternative views regarding the interpretation of a particular musical work, we are preparing to set our own goal and strategy for the interpretation of the music. Similarly, we create an environment for our students whereby they, too, can benefit from hearing different perspectives regarding a particular task at hand. As thoughts are shared in the rehearsal by one student they can become the impetus for extended metacognitive thinking by other students. Shared thinking about the rehearsal piece can result in a greater proliferation of ideas that spur each person's capacity to engage in metacognition as it relates to individual parts. As teachers and students share their thinking, their goals and strategies become mutually reinforcing and the rehearsal time may be used more efficiently.

The implications for involving students in critiquing their own rehearsal tapes are three-fold: (1) this involvement focuses attention on the relationship of individual parts to the piece as a whole; (2) it engages students in monitoring and evaluating their own progress as well as the progress of the group; and (3) it fosters personal commitment by making available opportunities for students to develop self-control by channeling their energies to attain a common goal, that is, getting the most out of rehearsal time and producing the best possible performance.

Creating

It is possible for students to sit through years of general music classes and never be asked to reflect upon a musical problem. One of the most important components of a creative music strategy—one that invites students to pose or solve a musical problem—is the degree to which we invite them to reflect upon their musical thought processes. Such questions as "How did you begin? How did you proceed? How did you make your decisions? Would you do anything differently next time?" encourage students to become aware of their own thinking.

It is easy to rely on familiar patterns and do "more of the same" when students move from one creative music strategy to another. By engaging them in "why," "how," and "what" questions, we encourage students to plan ahead, to monitor their own behavior and openly evaluate outcomes. By responding to such questions students begin to think about alternative ways of carrying out a task.

Tape recording and playing back the outcomes of students' creative endeavors provides the springboard upon which metacognitve thinking can occur. As in the evaluation component of the performance activity, it provides students with an opportunity to reflect upon their work. They aurally scrutinize the playback tape to determine the effectiveness of their musical choices.

After hearing the playback tape, their scrutiny is enhanced by questions to further the metacognitive thinking process. "What did you hear? How did it work in terms of your plan? What seemed to work best? Why did it work, or not work?" These questions help students translate their thoughts into words and make their thoughts more concrete and available to them for future reference.

What Brown (1978) refers to as conscious control of one's own activities is essential for all forms of knowing. "In the domain of deliberate learning and problem solving situations, conscious executive control of the routines available is the essence of intelligent activity" (79). Discussing the outcomes of a creative endeavor helps to highlight for students the available routines in the realm of musical choices. Checking the results of the endeavor against criteria of effectiveness is a metacognitive skill. Brown believes this is applicable whether the task under consideration is solving a math problem, memorizing a prose passage, following a recipe, or assembling an automobile (80).

Listening

It is fairly common to direct students' listening for particular musical content before they hear a new piece of music, for example, "Listen to the melody played by the brass; hear the countermelody in the violin section." It is also common practice to play a recording and then pose specific questions about the musical content of the piece, such as "Which instrument played the melody?" If we want to encourage metacognitive thinking during listening activities, we must create strategies that allow for a wide range of responses. Students stretch their ears when they believe what they hear will be valued.

One means for engaging students in the kind of listening that requires metacognitive thinking is to play an unfamiliar work for the purpose of generating *from* the students musical information about the piece.

Instead of focusing attention to specific musical details (of melody, rhythm, orchestration, and so forth), the teacher informs the students that they will be asked what they heard in the music. After listening, as they share their perceptions of the music (often in nonmusical terms), the teacher can attach appropriate terminology to their descriptions and provide notational references to render their descriptors in music-related vocabulary. With correct terminology and notational references on the chalkboard, students can monitor their ability to hear not only their original perceptions, but also the perceptions shared by other students.

When dealing with a piece of music relatively unfamiliar to the students, teachers can provide them with opportunities to use their emerging music-related vocabulary. The opportunities also assist and challenge students to think about what there is to know or hear in the music. The strategy provides the teacher with opportunities to teach and reinforce content and notational skills. Additionally, teachers are in a position to monitor student learnings. The students' metacognitive assessments can enhance the development of logical follow-up strategies.

The teacher's role is to present the music and invite students to share their aural perceptions by eliciting information about the ways in which the various elements of music function in the piece. The critical issue is that students become aware of what they actually hear and think about as they listen to music. Relying upon their own ears for gathering musical information encourages self-directed and autonomous listening. The implication for involving students in this aural, musical data collection, as noted earlier, is that they begin to see themselves as designers of their own learning.

Knowledge and Self Control

Paris and Winograd adopt the view that metacognition involves knowledge and control of self (cited in Marzano et al. 1988, 10). They point out three aspects of self-regulation that need to be controlled and monitored for metacognitive thinking to occur: commitment, attitude and attention. The authors believe that students can choose to be committed to a task, can elect to have positive attitudes about the task and can determine to be attentive to issues regarding the task. The wisdom that grows out of classroom teaching experience, however, suggests that, in order for this to happen, there is much to be facilitated by the teacher. As Holt (1964) astutely observes in the following illustration:

> A child is most intelligent when the reality before him arouses in him a high degree of attention, interest, concentration, involvement—in short, when he cares most about what he is doing. This is why we should make schoolrooms and schoolwork as interesting and exciting as possible, not just so that school will be a pleasant place, but so that children in school will act intelligently and get into the *habit* of acting intelligently (159).

We can't demand commitment from our students or require them to decide to put the necessary energies into a task. We can, however, help them learn about commitment by engaging them in a curriculum that is musically inviting and motivating, that requires them to think and take action, and that provides them with opportunities to participate in decision-making processes.

What might be the nature of such a curriculum? The words process-oriented, experiential, and generative come to mind. As I have written before, it

> emphasizes objectives that deal with assisting the learners in the discovery, acquisition, organization and application of musical information. It involves a learning program in which students interact with musical content as they assume the roles of composer, performer, conductor, critical listener and music researcher. The ongoing music experiences planned for the students by the music

teacher are primarily based on those processes indigenous to musical behavior and creative problem solving (Pogonowski 1985, 148).

A basic assumption underlying the curriculum is that much learning results from group interaction, group problem solving, group analysis, and group evaluation of experiences. These activities serve to foster metacognitive thinking because they require students' commitment, attention, and willingness to participate fully. By comparing their own reactions, understandings and interpretations of materials and concepts with those of others in the class, they are monitoring and controlling their own thinking.

Commitment, attention, and attitudes conducive to productive activity are the result of teaching strategies designed to give students a sense of ownership in the curriculum. For example, students' attitudes about themselves in music class and their attitudes about the value of specific classroom activities will influence their attention and commitment levels. In a recent study of children's musical thinking, I found in interviews with ten-year-old children that music class was most interesting when students were permitted to work in groups to create musical compositions. They enjoyed the opportunity this activity afforded them to independently make decisions and to see how their musical decisions were similar to or different from other peer groups. (Pogonowski, in press.)

Knowledge and Control of Process

The *Dimensions of Thinking* authors adopt the view that metacognition involves knowledge and control of process. They identify three types of knowledge that are important to metacognition: declarative, procedural and conditional.

Declarative knowledge has to do with facts. For example, I know that the bass drum has a low sound, the piano has a wide range, and that the first Prelude in Book I of *The Well-Tempered Clavier* is in the key of C Major. I know that organum is the name for the earliest types of polyphonic music, Haydn and Mozart wrote symphonies and string quartets, and that Phillip Glass is a prominent composer of minimal music in the second half of the twentieth century. Declarative knowledge can pertain to oneself as well. I know that my listening goals differ when I listen to popular music from when I listen to a Baroque fugue. When a student is aware of what he or she knows ("declares" to know), the student also has the advantage of knowing what he needs to know to complete a musical task. This advantage positions him to know what his limitations are and what questions to pose.

Procedural knowledge is the result of "knowing how." It is an outgrowth of direct experience with a variety of musical materials. It is the consequence of our explorations and interactions with timbre, tonal systems, rhythms, dynamics, and forms.

For example, I know how to conduct, to plan an improvisation, and to play three instruments. Each of these examples requires many operations. In order to conduct, I must know how to start and stop the group, how to convey my interpretation, and how to give effective cues for various entrances. Procedural knowledge refers to the myriad actions involved in performing any task, including how to get help when we don't know about a particular procedure. If a student is having trouble executing a passage on his or her trumpet, he or she may procedurally seek help by talking to the first chair or, as a result of her teacher's advice, look up alternative fingerings on a trumpet fingering chart.

Mature students can often find out "how" by asking questions, though much of "knowing how" in music grows out of the experiences we have *with* music. An important responsibility we share as teachers is to inform our students how to acknowledge what they need to know and then how to pursue appropriate avenues for satisfying the learning need.

Conditional knowledge, as identified by *Dimensions of Thinking* authors, refers "to knowing why a given strategy works or when to use one skill or strategy as opposed to another" (Marzano et al. 14). It involves knowing when one approach to solving a problem is more efficient than another. Conditional knowledge also helps us decide when a particular tactic is not working and an alternative must be sought.

Self- or group-interrogative procedures are useful for getting at the "when" and "why" questions. The following questions would apply in some creating activities: "When will you use silence? When will you introduce the second rhythm pattern? When do you plan to introduce the augmented sixth chord? When should we begin the crescendo?" Why could be substituted for the first word of each of these questions to get at the reasoning behind students' tactics and musical choices they make: "Why will you use silence? Why will you introduce the second rhythm pattern? Why do you plan to introduce the augmented sixth chord? Why should we begin the crescendo?"

According to the authors of *Dimensions of Thinking,* declarative, procedural and conditional knowledge are essential aspects of metacognition. It is important to identify the components of the three types of knowledge in order to monitor our own behavior as teachers when planning various musical activities for students. If we systematically reflect the three types of knowledge in the kinds of questions we pose and the activities we plan, we will be teaching and reinforcing metacognition for musical thinking.

Examples of the three types of knowledge important to metacognition can be seen if we look at some samples of probable thinking on the part of the teacher and of the student within the context of a single strategy. Let's assume one of the primary goals of the teacher's strategy is for students to become familiar with chords as preparation for creating progressions. In planning the strategy, the teacher employs the three types of knowledge to check his thinking regarding the appropriateness of the strategy or, said in another way, the teacher checks his thinking about the readiness of the students to successfully cope with the strategy. A capsulated view of the teacher's metacognitive process could reveal the following:

Declarative: "I know the students are aware of the potential of our classroom instruments from their previous experiences with them, that they are comfortable creating melodies on mallet and keyboard instruments, and that the students are relatively comfortable with the concept of chords as a result of our explorations and discussions of them in the previous two classes."

Procedural: "The students know *how* to build and label a chord from the root of the chord, *how* to check the accuracy of their thinking with other students or the teacher, and *how* to be mutually supportive as they work in dyads."

Conditional: "Even though the students have successfully created melodies and various effects on the instruments, they need experience creating chords beyond our initial explorations and discussions. They need to learn the most efficient means for accurately producing chords in order to make personally meaningful judgments concerning their use. If this strategy is successful, students will begin or continue to develop aural recognition of chords, dexterity in producing them, and vocabulary to describe them. Following their work in dyads, they will share the chords they found with the rest of the class. For future planning I will have to determine one of the following: (1) whether this strategy is sufficient for preparing them to create short chord progressions, (2) whether we need to continue with this strategy next time, or (3) whether a different preparatory strategy is in order."

A glimpse of a student's metacognitive thinking relative to the above could reveal the following trains of thought:

Declarative: "I *know* from our class activities and discussions what a chord is, that it has three members, and that the lowest member is its name when I use every other bar on the xylophone."

Procedural: "I know *how* to play each of the chord members separately and my teacher tells me I am then playing arpeggiated chords. What I need to figure out is how to play each of the chord members simultaneously. I found out *how* to put two mallets in my right hand and one mallet in my left hand to play a chord. I also found out *how* a three-pronged mallet works with just one hand.

Conditional: "Now that I know how to play chords in three different ways, I am ready to experiment and decide which chords I will share with the class. I also have to decide whether I am going to play the chords in only one way or to demonstrate the three different ways I am learning."

Executive Control

Executive control as defined by the authors of *Dimensions of Thinking* is "evaluating, planning and regulating the declarative, procedural and conditional information involved in a task (144). It is the second aspect of metacognition that relates to knowledge and control of process.

Costa (1984) suggests that students be made aware of their metacognitive abilities by thinking of a task as having *before, during* and *after* components (58–59). In a creative music strategy, *before* can be facilitated by teachers pointing out steps for approaching a problem, rules to remember, time constraints, available materials or instruments, and any other relevant information that provides students with guidelines or criteria. These criteria are then available for evaluating, planning and regulating their performance all along the musical task continuum.

With criteria established, students can begin to determine what musical facts may bear upon the task at hand (declarative knowledge), what they will need to be able to do in order to realize their ideas or goals (procedural knowledge), and how to accomplish their goals as efficiently as possible (conditional knowledge).

Let us suppose the students in groups of five are gong to create a rhythm piece by varying a given two-measure eighth-note pattern. Prior to working on this task the teacher models some metacognitive thinking to provide students with questions to ask themselves before, during, and after the task has been completed.

Before the small group task, the teacher and students perform the eighth-note pattern without any expressive concerns. Mutually, they note "how uninteresting" the pattern sounds. "What musical treatments could we consider to make the pattern interesting?" Students respond with suggestions having to do with a variety of dynamics, changing timbres, and the use of rests for occasional silences. A series of "Who knows how..." questions invites volunteers to demonstrate one or another musical treatment. "When" and "why" questions follow and a number of ideas are generated for planning considerations.

18

As the teacher is modeling metacognitive thinking, the students are challenged to think about "why, how, and when." They are evaluating their own and each other's suggestions, planning how the musical ideas might work in their small group pieces and regulating their thinking about what they might be able to use, given their own limitations.

Evaluation, planning and regulation before the task has to do with "what" and "how" will it sound? Do we begin with a triangle or do we begin with a bass drum? What is the consequence of either choice for achieving the desired result?" Evaluation, planning and regulation in the "before" stage is speculative. Students weigh alternative musical hypotheses in preparation for their musical plan.

During the small group activity, Costa (1984) recommends that teachers circulate among the groups and "invite students to share their progress, thought processes and perceptions..." about the developing rhythm piece (59). Asking students to indicate how far they are into their pieces, to describe their "trail of thinking up to that point," and to define how they intended to pursue the remainder of the piece helps them become aware of their own behavior. As Costa observes, "It also provides teachers with a diagnostic cognitive map of students' thinking, which can be used to give more individualized assistance" (59).

After involves assessment of and knowledge about the musical content in the group rhythm pieces. As students listen to each other's works, they should be encouraged to verbalize about the musical techniques they hear, about the techniques they enjoy the most, or think are particularly effective, and about musical ideas for future projects. Discussions of this nature will assist students in gaining knowledge and control of process. "After" also involves assessment of their work patterns: "Did they utilize time wisely? Were they cooperative with their group? Did they stay on task?" These and similar questions will help students learn to monitor and regulate their behavior and in the process gain knowledge and control of self.

We have to infuse metacognitive strategies into our teaching methods if, as a significant outcome of music education, we wish to develop independent musical thinkers. This means we need to consciously assist students in monitoring their thinking behavior as they interact with music, so that they eventually regulate and control their behavior themselves. It's not our monitoring their behavior in the traditional "disciplinarian" sense that will make the difference. Raising their consciousness with monitoring strategies that encourage students to approach musical tasks with deliberation, purpose, awareness, and control *will* make the difference!

3

CRITICAL AND CREATIVE MUSICAL THINKING

MARK DETURK

Dimensions of Thinking properly stresses the complementary nature of critical and creative thinking; however, in music these two terms seem to have more specialized connotations than they do in many other subject areas. Because of this, attention will be directed here to the uniqueness of each. Though the products of each kind of thought may be different, the curricular impact of a concern for thinking of any kind should be the same—making room in the curriculum for teaching, modeling, practicing, and evaluating thinking.

Critical Thinking about Music

Critical thinking about music enjoys a long and cherished history in musical life. Evaluation is a primary goal of critical thinking, and music is evaluated in cognitive and affective ways that are informed by experience. "Critical thinking is the result of experiential learning that embraces the

21

learner's affective and cognitive domains" (Pogonowski 1987, 38).

Hudgins and Edelman (1986, 333) define a good critical thinker as one with "the disposition to provide evidence in supporting one's conclusions and to request evidence from others before accepting their conclusions." Good critical thinkers about music rely upon conceptual musical evidence as the basis for their evaluations. They critically evaluate a particular work by understanding the music and the merits of its parts and its totality. In this way evaluation is derived from musical evidence rather than from peer pressure, whim, or fashion.

Music makes three demands on the good critical thinker. First is a conceptual knowledge of music: The critical thinker must understand the elements of music. Second is a storehouse of musical experience which serves as a yardstick against which other music is measured both affectively and cognitively: The critical thinker must have high quality resources available for comparison. Third is a metacognitive strategy or "disposition" (Ennis 1987, 10) to seek musical evidence as the basis for musical evaluation: The critical thinker must wish to, and know how to, make an informed decision.

Critical Thinking in the Music Curriculum

Critical or evaluative thinking has been commonly listed as an important educational goal (Bloom et al. 1956). Likewise, high level thinking has long been stated as a broadly held goal in music education. The *Resolution on the Creative Arts* adopted by the American Association of School Administrators in 1959 proclaimed, "It is important that pupils, as a part of general education learn to appreciate, to understand, to create, and *to criticize with discrimination* [emphasis added] those products of the mind, the voice, the hand, and the body which give dignity to the person and exalt the spirit of man" (Ernst and Gary 1965, 1).

Over the past thirty years teachers have been urged to prepare their students to do the following:

1. "Compare musical styles ranging from serious masterworks to jazz classics. They should also prize quality renditions of music" (Leonhard and House 1959, 184).

2. "Discriminate with respect to music" (Ernst and Gary 1965, 11)

3 "Examine the criteria employed in making value judgments about music" (Schwadron 1967, 79)

4. Perform "acts of decision making, judging, or selecting based on a given set of criteria. As an example, using specific criteria other than emotional inclination, the music learner evaluates a musical composition new to him" (Sidnell 1973, 70–71).

5. "Make judgments about music, and value the personal worth of music" (First National Assessment of Educational Progress 1970, 16).

6. Develop the "aesthetic judgment and aesthetic value... [necessary] in formulating judgments regarding the use and quality of music" (Abeles, Klotman and Hoffer 1984, 95).

Teaching Critical Thinking about Music

Instruction must prepare the student for each of the three requirements of musical critical thinking. First, *The critical thinker must understand the elements of music*. Attention should be devoted to acquiring and relating the basic concepts of music and its performance. People need to understand the cognitively low level concepts of timbre, tempo, dynamics and simple melody and rhythm as well as the middle and higher level relational concepts of complex melody and rhythm, harmony, tonality, form, texture, and expressiveness. They also need to gain various levels of performance concepts with regard to tone quality, accuracy of pitch and rhythm, ensemble, and personal sensitivity. Well-taught students know these concepts and the labels that make them useful and retrievable. These same students display their conceptual knowledge as they perform, describe, and create music.

People must be able to employ their concepts of the elements of music and quality performance as the basis for evaluation. The curriculum at every level should include some attention to each. Elementary general music instruction ought to include the performance concepts of good tone production, intonation, ensemble, and expression, along with its emphasis on the elements of music. Secondary school performance teachers must not abandon teaching the concepts of music as the basis for critical thinking when describing or creating as well as when performing music.

Second, *the critical thinker must have high-quality resources available for comparison*. Through experience with a rich resource of music of all kinds students acquire a personal storehouse of music that serves as a background against which evaluation is performed. Music classes should provide ever deeper and broader musical experiences that students can make their own.

Two concerns are obvious. One is that the music teachers supply in class needs to be of high quality if it is to serve effectively for the purpose of comparison. The importance of quality literature as the vehicle of study and experience cannot be over-emphasized. Both general music and performance teachers should constantly check to ascertain if their selections meet this requirement. The demands of entertaining general music students or performance group audiences often tempt teachers to devote time to music of lesser value.

Teachers need to defend the selection of literature as a primary issue in curriculum decision making.

Another concern is that the most noteworthy elements of that high-quality music studied need to be labeled and have attention drawn to them. Without labeling, much of the musical material in memory may be irretrievable. For example, students can be directed to sections of works by name rather than by rehearsal number. "Let's begin at the second theme, please" involves a great deal more conceptual learning than "Let's begin at measure thirty-seven." Likewise, tonalities are minor, not sad. Pitches are out of tune, not sour.

Third, *the critical thinker must wish to, and know how to, make an informed decision.* The habit of relying upon concept knowledge and stored musical experience as the basis for musical evaluation must be established. Transfer of learning cannot be assumed. Students need to hear unfamiliar music, be encouraged to discuss it in elemental musical terms, and compare it to other works on those terms, as well as on affective terms. Teachers might begin conversations about pieces by asking students first to describe those instruments or voices involved. This may be followed by accurately representing themes (melody), motivic rhythm and other rhythm characteristics, and tempo. Finally, attention may be paid to group considerations of key (harmony), form, and style. Only after music can be accurately described can it be convincingly evaluated. Comparison with other known works and discussion of composer's intent represent still higher levels of critical thinking.

Students can be exposed to the critical thinking of others and asked to respond to it in a way that will make them sensitive to the need for supportive conceptual evidence as the basis for criticism. They can be asked to argue for and against the merits of particular pieces or of performances, orally or in writing. Asking students to evaluate the quality of some other person's critical thoughts provides a valuable detached view of the process just as editing someone else's writing provides a detached view of the composition process.

Evaluating Critical Thinking About Music

Evaluating higher-level thinking skills has always been a problem for teachers. It is a difficult task that seems to defy efficient group solutions. This is one reason that so much teaching is directed instead at lower-level learning—it is easy to test. Music teachers, however, are especially familiar with the argument that something can be worth teaching and learning even if it is difficult to test. Like the subject of music itself, critical thinking about music is worth teaching, though evaluation can be elusive.

The evaluation of critical thinking skills is best accomplished by confronting students with evaluation tasks and observing the results. In this sense the teaching procedure and the evaluation procedure are similar. Further, evaluation of students' critical thinking serves to continually redirect the teaching effort toward the lower-level learning objectives. Critical thinking evaluations almost always point up areas of conceptual weakness and send the teacher off to strengthen these areas and then reevaluate the thinking process.

Critical thinking is not easily evaluated by the traditional format of standardized, short-answer examinations. Obtaining a correct answer is not the real assignment for the student in a thinking evaluation. Instead, the goal for students (as clearly communicated by the teacher) should be to display their thought processes. Students can do this through written essays or personal interviews. This allows for the evaluation of the process itself. According to Hudgins (1966, 11), "Directions which many teachers give to their pupils to 'show your work' or to 'explain why you chose' a particular alternative seem well advised. Such explanations provide the teacher with information which bears directly upon the pupils' processes of thinking."

Even when essay tests have successfully elicited from students the thought processes employed, there has always been the problem of finding a reliable method for assessing those essays. One method of ranking essays with some proven success (DeTurk 1988a) involves the rating of student thinking via the SOLO Taxonomy (Biggs and Collis 1982). It is the accuracy and sophistication of the thinking *process,* not the correctness of any final conclusion, that is evaluated.

According to this procedure, students are asked to write an essay in which they describe, analyze, and evaluate in musical terms a composition heard or performed. Those essays are then assigned to one of five categories based upon their content and structure. These categories represent increasingly sophisticated levels of critical thinking reflecting conceptual knowledge and its structure. They are described below with illustrative excerpts from sample student essays.

1. Prestructural essays display no structured learning of the subject and typically avoid, deny or simply fail to respond accurately to the assignment. (Notice that evaluations based on non-musical concepts fall within this category.) *Example:* "The first piece of music makes me feel dominant, triumphant.... The second piece makes me feel carefree like taking a trip to an exotic island.... The evil in the first song and the happiness in the second song is why they are different." (No musical concept cited.)

2. Unistructural essays rely upon a single lower-level musical concept or fact (simple rhythm, tempo, dynamics, or performance medium) as the basis

for unsophisticated conclusions reached hastily. *Example:* "The first piece of music had a very heavy, strong beat.... The second piece had a much lighter beat with a more positive attitude.... I don't think one is any better than the other." (Single music concept cited: rhythmic stress)

3. Multistructural essays employ several not well unified musical concepts or facts of the same type as unistructural essays. They seek multiple evidence but do not present a unified argument. *Example:* "The first piece starts out loud and gets softer right away. There are people singing in it.... It sounds like the music is being played by string instruments.... The second piece starts out with real slow music played by string instruments. As it goes on it gets faster and a flute is heard.... Both pieces have a lot of different instruments in them. The first piece goes from loud to soft a lot, but the second one stays pretty much the same." (Three music concepts cited: dynamics, instrumentation, tempo.)

4. Relational essays display both a grasp of higher level concepts (such as form, orchestration, style) and present unified arguments that successfully incorporate evidence from several concepts into convincing answers that deal with the assignments as narrowly defined. *Example:* "The second piece is more contemporary than the first. The choir leads the first piece, in comparison to just one singer leading the second piece. Instrumentally, they were also different. The first had more of an orchestra sound to it. The second had more of a jazzy band sound to it.... The first began loud and harsh, the second began with a warm and flowing tone. Both pieces had different sections or forms within them. I thought the quality of both pieces was very good. I tend to like the second piece better because of the more contemporary sound." (Four lower music concepts cited: instrumentation, medium, dynamics and timbre. Two higher music concepts cited: form, historical style period.)

5. Extended abstract essays: "The first piece has three sections. The first section is a full orchestra playing long, full chords, is forte and has a minor sound.... The second piece has two sections. The first is gentle and relaxed, the second is jazzier and more upbeat. The sax, bass and drums provide a happy dancing beat.... These two pieces each have a different purpose.... For this reason they are hard to compare. Each completes its mission." (Three lower music concepts cited: medium, dynamics, and tempo. Three higher music concepts cited: form, tonality, musical function. Discussion of musical purpose [function] exceeds the bounds of the assignment.)

The reliability of the SOLO Taxonomy across subject disciplines has proven to be quite high (Biggs and Collis, 187–89). In a study of 279 critical essays about music written by high school juniors and rated by three different readers, reliability was .89. For only fourteen (5 percent) of the essays were those readers unable to reach agreement as to what level rating was appropriate. Each judge felt the ratings were valid in representing the students' abilities to think critically about music. One reader altered her approach to teaching as a result of the insight gained from this evaluation procedure (DeTurk 1988b, 68–69).

Creative Thinking about Music

Like critical thinking, creative thinking is higher-level thinking with a specialized purpose—the production of something new. The focus on "output" separates creative thinking from problem solving, another advanced thinking skill. For instance, problem solving might lead to the conclusion that creative thought was necessary for some purpose.

Eisner (1964, 10) quotes Morris Stein's definition of a creative product as "a novel work that is considered useful, tenable, or satisfying by some group at some point in time." Creative musical thinking most often involves the unique, personal manipulation of the materials of music as currently understood by the creative thinker. For serious art works such manipulation is generally thought to be both original and expressive in nature.

The authors of *Dimensions of Thinking* outline five aspects of creative thinking which are reviewed here with respect to music.

1. Creativity takes place in conjunction with intense desire and preparation. Motivation to create must be strong enough to see students through to the completion of the task. Persistence, often used as a measure of motivation, is a prerequisite for and one indicator of creative thinking. Students are most persistent at creative thinking projects that they value themselves. Assignments of a four-part chorale for piano may not motivate every student!

If creative thinking requires precise, intense, and prolonged involvement with an objective, then class curricula need to suggest, require, value, and reward that kind of effort in and of itself. Further, meaningful results can be expected to develop only over an extended period.

2. Creativity involves working at the edge rather than at the center of one's capacity. Creative thinkers often test their abilities and seek new knowledge in the process of creating. By accepting a creative task they subject themselves to an endeavor whose demands are not entirely known to them in advance. They are, therefore, risk takers in pursuit of their objective. For some students the risk itself motivates. For others it provides an excuse for failure. For most it is an element that must be monitored and controlled.

Having once assigned or encouraged creative thought, it is important to make assignments that fall within the overlap of the attainable and the chal-

27

lenging. Most people willingly accept and derive satisfaction from assignments with a moderate level of difficulty and risk.

3. Creativity requires an internal rather than external locus of evaluation. Working to personal standards in pursuit of a personal product serves to isolate the creative thinker from peer pressure and possibly even teacher evaluation. This can be threatening to the classroom teacher who feels accountable to the schools and parents for the nature and quality of student work. Yet everything we know about creative individuals points to their own individual, intrinsic set of values.

To encourage internal evaluation the teacher is well advised to value and assist students with the *process* of creation rather than focus exclusively on an evaluation of the product. In this way the student may welcome experienced advice especially with the execution of detail. Young students can be shown how to create songs from short rhythm and melody patterns they find in speech, prose and poetry. Improvisers can be shown how to alter melodic motives to create unique solos. Composers may need help notating music, writing appropriately for instruments and voices, finding compatible voice combinations, and arranging performances. The teacher might direct students toward computer programs that allow them to compose and then hear the results of their efforts.

4. Creativity involves reframing ideas. There are many similar terms for this reframing process. Divergent, fluid, flexible, metaphoric, and lateral thinking all share a focus on developing alternative approaches. These terms imply the creation of new schemas or thought patterns that lead to original paradigms, style practices, musical genres, and theories. Such thinking requires tremendous time and concentration and probably is not realistic as a limited classroom objective.

Eisner (1964, 10) labels this type of creative thinking aesthetic organization. It is thinking focused upon creating something beautiful, and he argues that it is a special domain for thinkers in the arts. Its method is to organize ideas, actions, or qualities into aesthetically pleasing wholes. This focus is on creativity, the aesthetic arrangement of the elements of music, within a given schema. Students can work successfully at this task of composition and improvisation.

5. Creativity can sometimes be facilitated by getting away from intensive engagement for awhile to permit free-flowing thought. Whatever the mechanism is for the "Oh, my gosh!" experience in which a revelation is received, its implications for the classroom teacher are limited. If students need time away from projects to allow for "thought fermentation" it might be suggested that their work be given a due date, and then returned for improvements at a later

time. Meeting a due date is, after all, a professional creativity requirement of the first magnitude.

Creative Thinking in the Music Curriculum

It is strangely true that few music courses are structured to include teaching creative thinking. Creativity is rarely encouraged in this subject, the most abstract of the creative arts. Nonetheless, teaching creative thinking in the creative arts has been espoused regularly as natural and appropriate. Further, the recent increase in concern for creative thinking in all subjects has benefitted music in particular.

Leonhard and House urge the music teacher to *"emphasize creativity in all music instruction"* [emphasis theirs] (1959, 260). Hoffer (1973, 58) feels that "Musical learning should not be confined to the recreation of what others have done. At a level consistent with their musical sophistication, students should engage in creating music through composition or improvisation, or both." Abeles, Hoffer, and Klotman write that "creative activities are undertaken because the act of creating is itself of value to the students" (1984, 152).

While these and similar sentiments from reputable music educators abound, there seems to be less consensus about teaching creative thinking than there is about teaching critical thinking. This is true for education in general as well as for music education in particular. In the past students have been encouraged to understand creative thinking rather than taught to do it. Studies of the thinking of master composers have been common. During this century articles and books reporting the thought processes of respected musical creators (such as Leonard Bernstein, Aaron Copland, Roger Sessions, or Igor Stravinsky) have been very popular. Recognition and appreciation of creative thinking in others can be strengthened, however, by doing it.

At the least an effort should be made to structure music courses so as not to block creative efforts. The curriculum ought to contain the flexibility to allow for creative exploration. Music classes, especially at the secondary level, often appear to be among the most rigidly structured in the schools. That very structure may discourage the learner with a personal objective to pursue. Further, the extreme demands of many performance classes simply prohibit students from devoting attention and energy to the creation of music. Should it surprise us to find that, for these and other reasons, the most musically creative students in our schools often avoid music classes?

Teaching Creative Musical Thinking

Methodology for the teaching of creativity is controversial. A variety of opinions can be found to such basic issues as at what age to begin, how much structure to build into the experience, and even what it means to *teach* creative thinking. As pointed out in *Dimensions of Thinking*, however, creative and critical thinking are similar processes and might be expected to benefit from a similar progression of instruction.

1. The creative thinker must understand the elements of music. Like critical thinking, creative thinking requires a knowledge of and curiosity about the elements of music. The circular nature of this relationship means that creative work should send the student back to further understand the concepts of music, thus reinforcing and expanding earlier learning. Curricula such as the *Manhattanville Music Curriculum Project* (Thomas 1970) are constructed upon this reciprocal relationship between basic knowledge and creativity.

2. The creative thinker must have high-quality resources available for comparison. Creative thinking often operates like a metaphor. The thinker may wonder, "Can I do something like the piece I heard yesterday?" This kind of thought requires a resource of musical works with which to draw parallels. Teachers who teach high-quality music to their students prepare them to think creatively. By labeling the musical elements and forms of those works studied the teacher makes them even more available to students.

3. The creative thinker must wish to, and know how to, carry out the process of production. Though established composers and improvisers may cite an internal need to express themselves, the disposition to create is probably not inborn. Students need motivation in the form of encouragement, modeling, and valuing of the creative effort from their teachers. Room must be made in the daily musical life for discussion of, and attempts at, creativity. Finally, teachers must make available to their students assistance with the craft of musical creation.

Evaluating Creative Thinking about Music

The fact that creators usually work with reference to their own evaluative criteria has been previously mentioned. This does not preclude a teacher from making informed assessments of a student's creative thinking efforts. The personal nature of creative thinking almost dictates that assessment be made on an individual basis. The time consuming nature of this kind of evaluation may be one of the reasons that instruction in creativity is not more common.

Studies often mention three different aspects of creativity: process, product, and characteristics of the individual. Only the first two aspects are appropriate for evaluation in the schools since the third does not vary as a result of instruction. The product (the composition) is worthy of evaluation since good process (creative thinking) normally bears a commensurate product. Process information is most valuable for the design of further instruction and requires regular individual consultation with the student.

Kratus (1988) presents a series of evaluation scales, checklists, and data collection techniques for assessing the processes and products of creative thinking rather than the traits of the creative thinker. He defends their validity, reliability, and reasonableness as methods of use to teachers. "By focusing on process or product instead of person, measurement can more directly measure a music lesson's objectives or a music program's goals in terms of student behavior in specific activities" (13). He emphasizes procedures and grading scales that evaluate both the musical characteristics and the creative characteristics of creative processes and products.

Implications

Raising a concern for musical thinking skills has several implications for the teaching of music that might cause educators to reflect upon their own teaching, their own student experiences and how research informs us about music learning.

1. Musical thinking skills are included among the objectives listed in most books and articles written about music education during this century. An examination of these materials will reveal a priority placed upon the development of thinking skills useful in adult life for choosing, evaluating, and creating music to perform or hear. Teaching students higher-order thinking skills is not a new or temporary concern.

2. Performing ensembles perform in a superior fashion if their curriculum includes attention to broad musical learnings other than rehearsal. Studies have shown that rates (of both listening skills and group festival performances) improve for groups and the individual students involved who are taught to think about music rather than just rehearse it.

3. The public, with or without personal school musical experience, routinely is critical of school music education for not teaching the subject of music at a level useful for adults. The ongoing need to defend teaching music in school may be the result of the general population's memory of music instruction that failed to prepare it to think about music in a sophisticated manner.

4. When asked to list those musical topics about which they were curious, students frequently mention composition, orchestration, and improvisation. Student desire for advanced instruction of this type is often ignored by teachers. There appears to be a student population with the interests and abilities to pursue such subjects, which require higher-level musical thinking.

5. What is good for the best, is good for the rest. Current education thinking

holds that if we can identify elements of the curriculum that are beneficial for the most advanced students we ought to ask sincerely if they should not be taught to all. If higher-level thinking is a valuable skill to foster and encourage for some, then perhaps it should be a part of each student's course of study. Following such a line of thought relieves teachers of the arbitrary task of identifying particular students as especially deserving of such instruction.

6. Teachers need to be able to assume different roles. Some discomfort may arise from the need to serve as maestro for students when rehearsing, virtuoso when teaching the instrument or voice, and coach when encouraging higher-level thinking. Especially when thinking creatively, students may have valid thoughts quite different from our own. Here, more than anywhere else, exists the possibility of finding students more skillful than ourselves. Good teachers recognize and encourage those students without feeling threatened.

4

MUSICAL THINKING PROCESSES

BRIAN MOORE

In the real world, we do not think just for the sake of thinking; we think about something. Problems are seldom solved simply for the experience of solving problems. Decision making is not an isolated process but is interwoven with a topic or subject. Whether casting a vote for a presidential candidate or deciding how to end a musical phrase, our knowledge and experience form a contextual framework for our thinking.

Review of *Dimensions of Thinking*

Dimensions of Thinking identifies eight thinking processes that are frequently mentioned in the literature and are fundamental for achieving goals in educational and real world situations. These eight processes are conceived in two categories: Knowledge Acquisition and Knowledge Production or Application. Since any specific thinking process interacts with each of the other seven, thinking is viewed from a multi-dimensional perspective. Thinking processes should thus be conceived as a network rather than a hierarchy (Marzano et al., 33). The eight processes identified in *Dimensions of Thinking* are:

1. Concept Formation—organizing information about an entity and associating that information with a label (word).
2. Principle Formation—recognizing a relationship between or among concepts.
3. Comprehending—generating meaning or understanding by relating new information to prior knowledge.
4. Problem Solving—analyzing and resolving a perplexing or difficult situation.
5. Decision Making—selecting from among alternatives.
6. Research—conducting scientific inquiry.
7. Composing—developing a product, which may be written, musical, mechanical, or artistic.
8. Oral Discourse—talking with other people.

The authors of *Dimensions of Thinking* suggest that these processes should be thought of as repertoires rather than rigid sequences of core skills. While this may appear to inhibit a concise and clear-cut approach toward developing thinking in educational settings, an understanding of this network of processes can and must affect our view of curriculum, learning, and teaching.

The Context for Thinking Processes in Music

While these processes are not new ideas for most educators, as defined by the authors of *Dimensions of Thinking,* implicit and explicit assumptions are made which impact on the interaction of musical content with thinking processes. An understanding of these assumptions—the context of each process—will assist toward developing a working model for musical thinking.

Concept Formation. As defined by Klausmeier (1985, 276), a "concept consists of a person's organized information about...objects, events, ideas, or processes—that enable the individual to discriminate the particular entity...and also to relate it to other entities and classes of entities." This view embraces language as the cornerstone of concept formation as vocabulary becomes the outward indication of a learner's grasp and understanding of a concept.

Klausmeier developed an instructional model for concept formation involving three phases: (1) concrete and identity levels, (2) beginning classificatory level, and (3) mature classificatory and formal levels. At the concrete and identity levels, the student is able to identify the same item, regardless of its context, as the target concept. The student who can identify the sound of a trumpet both with and without piano accompaniment as examples of "brass timbre" is operating at the identity level.

At the classificatory level, the learner can discriminate between examples and nonexamples of the concept and can begin to name its important features or attributes. At this level, a student would be able to recognize the sound of both a tuba and trumpet as examples of brass timbre and a clarinet as an example of nonbrass timbre.

At the formal level the student can note the salient features most often associated with the concept and can articulate a strategy for identifying both examples and nonexamples. The learner is also aware of how the concept in question relates to other concepts. Learners demonstrate conceptual understanding at the formal level primarily through the use of oral and written language. The student who has developed the formal concept of brass timbre is not only able to identify a clarinet as having a nonbrass timbre, but to describe the distinctive characteristics of a brass sound and verbalize the strategy used to aurally discriminate between various examples of brass and nonbrass timbres.

Given the importance of language in this model of concept formation, it would follow that to develop musical concepts, we must have a vocabulary that relates not only to text, but also to musical sound. Many music teachers, let alone music students, would have difficulty putting into written or spoken word the distinguishing features of concepts such as timbre. The use of musical sound to express and communicate conceptual understanding directly is an important instructional consideration.

This model of concept formation presupposes an understanding of the nature and structure of a discipline, because the formal level involves recognizing the relationships between concepts and their interconnective network.

Principle Formation. The authors of *Dimensions of Thinking* (42) note that the "goal of teaching principles is for students to *recognize* and *apply* the relationships...." The process of principle formation thus carries the same assumptions regarding a content area as does concept formation—that of an understanding of the nature of the discipline. While various kinds of principles exist (such as cause and effect and probability), it is the *fundamental* that has the greatest impact on the arts.

Fundamentals are universally accepted principles that characterize the ways information is organized within a discipline. Examples of musical fundamentals would be that melody implies harmony or that rhythm involves sound and silence.

The relationship between concepts and fundamentals (principles) is strong

35

and obvious: Fundamentals describe the organization of concepts within the art form we call music.

Comprehension. Comprehension is the process of gaining new knowledge. It is important to note that comprehension is a subjective process involving the *interpretation* of information. When presented with new content, the learner must make meaning through the conscious or unconscious selection of prior experience and current knowledge.

Most work in the study of comprehension in education has focused on reading comprehension. *Dimensions of Thinking* (44) presents an adaptation of a model for developing comprehension strategies in reading and listening to a text. This model (figure 1) can be further adapted for music listening.

Problem Solving. Perhaps the most important assumption concerning the process of problem solving is also the most obvious—a problem must exist. One interesting difference between novice and expert thinking is that experts are much more likely to notice problems in their area of expertise than are amateurs or novices. Many times in education however, problems presented to students are artificial since they are well structured and well defined. In the real world, such neat packaging does not exist.

Students need experience and practice with two types of problems: well defined and ill defined.

Various kinds of problem-solving strategies exist. Common characteristics include identifying the problem, defining and exploring multiple solutions and approaches, and looking at the results of one's efforts. A major attribute of problem solving is that of flexibility in thinking. Instructional strategies stress approaches that require the individual to perceive the problem from diverse perspectives. Imagery, analogies, and metaphors are suggested as ways of gaining this contrast in perception and perspective.

Such flexibility in the process of problem solving suggests an important instructional consideration: the availability of alternatives. In order for an individual to be flexible, options must be available. The teacher must be able to present both well-structured and ill-defined problems coupled with multiple models and strategies for their solution.

Problem solving in education has historically been in the domain of mathematics and science. The identification of problems and provision of multiple models for their solution is a perplexing one for music. Music educators are not trained to help students solve musical problems, let alone identify them. Even in instrumental and choral ensembles, the identification of performance problems and the selection of one solution from multiple models is usually done by the teacher alone. Students are seldom presented with musical prob-

Comprehension Strategies—Reading	Comprehension Strategies—Music

Before Reading/Listening
1. Preview the Information.
  • Survey the text features (title, subtitles, and graphics) or the preliminary information.
  • Survey the organizational patterns.
  • Survey the content focus.
2. Activate/Access Prior Knowledge.
  • Recall content and vocabulary.
  • Recall relevant categories of information and organizational patterns.
3. Focus Interest/Set Purposes.
  • Ask questions.
  • Predict content and organizational patterns.
	Before Listening
	1. Preview the Information.
	  • Survey the musical features (title, instrumentation, style, text) or any preliminary information.
	  • Survey the organizational patterns.
	  • Survey the focus of the musical content.
	2. Activate/Access Prior Knowledge.
	  • Recall musical content and aural vocabulary (i.e., timbres heard in previous music).
	  • Recall relevant categories of information and aural organizational patterns.
	3. Focus Interest/Set Purposes.
	  • Ask questions.
	  • Predict aural content (what will be heard) and organizational patterns.

During Reading/Listening
1. Confirm/Reject Predictions.
  • Assimilate new ideas.
  • Withhold judgment.
2. Clarify Ideas.
  • Attend to key vocabulary.
  • Generate new questions.
  • Evaluate ideas.
3. Construct Meaning for Each Segment of Information.
  • Select important ideas.
  • Connect and organize ideas.
	During Listening
	1. Confirm/Reject Predictions.
	  • Assimilate new ideas.
	  • Withhold judgment.
	2. Clarify Ideas.
	  • Attend to key aural events (aural vocabulary).
	  • Generate new questions.
	  • Evaluate ideas.
	3. Construct Meaning for Each Segment of Information.
	  • Select important ideas.
	  • Connect and organize ideas.

After Reading/Listening
1. Construct Meaning for the Information as a Whole.
  • Categorize/integrate information.
  • Summarize key ideas and their connection.
2. Assess Achievement of Purpose.
  • Confirm predictions.
  • Identify gaps in learning.
  • Extend learning to answer new questions/fill in gaps.
3. Consolidate/Apply Learning.
  • Transfer to new situations.
  • Rehearse and study.
	After Listening
	1. Construct Meaning for the Information as a Whole.
	  • Categorize/integrate aural information.
	  • Summarize key ideas and their connection.
	2. Assess Achievement of Purpose.
	  • Confirm predictions.
	  • Identify gaps in learning.
	  • Extend learning to answer new questions/fill in gaps.
	3. Consolidate/Apply Learning.
	  • Transfer to new situations.
	  • Rehearse and study.

Figure 1. Interrelation of thinking processes

lems to solve within the rehearsal.

If the thinking processes of students are to be developed, the music educator must be able to present learners with opportunities to work with well-structured and ill-defined problems within the context of *both* the rehearsal hall and music classroom.

Decision Making. Decision making is closely linked to problem solving and indeed could be argued as a kind of problem solving. Decisions always involve at least two competing alternatives that may or may not be obvious to the individual. The challenge is to select one of these alternatives by considering some criteria or goal. As with problem solving, various models with implications for instruction have been developed and several are presented in *Dimensions of Thinking.* Important characteristics of these models include the careful and complete defining of the goal, generation of ideas and alternative, evaluation of possible outcomes for each alternative, and selection of the alternative that is to be acted upon.

A contextual consideration is the goal or objective that forces the need for a decision to be made. The actual process of making a decision involves much verbal communication between teacher and student and among the students themselves. This process takes time to develop.

In the music classroom, the development of the decision making process must revolve around musical options and choices. The necessity of a vocabulary for the discussion of the content of music, previously mentioned in the section on concept development, is of equal importance here. The learner must be presented with problems and plausible models for their solution. For verbal discussion to occur between teacher and students, a common ground that includes the means for clear dialogue in the subject matter of music must exist. Oral and written language by itself do not suffice. The music student needs to be able to make choices and evaluate the results before any meaningful discussion can occur. Music educators have long provided their students with opportunities to experiences music as listeners and performers. Now we must make conscious instructional efforts to turn these passive experiences into active environments that encourage students to make decision and develop their musical thinking processes.

Research. Dimensions of Thinking defines research as scientific inquiry— that seeks to explain and predict. This is in contrast to problem solving or decision making where the goal is finding the right answer or solution. While this view of research has its roots in the natural and physical sciences, it should not be implied that the arts lack the need or potential for the development of such thinking. A broader view should be taken beginning with a more global definition for research—that of *systematic* inquiry.

The hallmarks of research are three-fold: (1) identification of a problem or problem area by observing and describing phenomena, (2) formulating hypotheses, and (3) testing and checking hypotheses. Each of these facets draws on other thinking processes.

1. Observing and describing phenomena involves perceiving what is new and relating it to what is known. This obviously calls upon the thinking process of comprehension and asks the researcher to categorize what is observed to allow it to be integrated in the existing knowledge base. This particular skill is crucial for the next phase in the research process, formulation of hypotheses.

2. The authors of *Dimensions of Thinking* note that "scientific thinking is a function of imagery, analogy and metaphor, as well as logical reasoning, any of which can be used to generate and evaluate mental models." A close connection exists between describing phenomena and formulating hypotheses because of the need to *select* observations. Raw observation without a contextual framework becomes meaningless. The researcher must continually call upon other thinking processes and skills (such as principle formation, comprehension, observing, or recall) to mold the models that will develop into hypotheses.

3. The purpose of testing is to either accept (confirm that theory supports observation) or reject (confirm that theory is *not* consistent with observation) the hypothesis in question. The actual procedures for carrying this out involve systematic collection and analysis of data. Experimental research relies heavily on test results where variables are manipulated and controlled. In contrast, ethnographic study focuses on observations in natural settings where variables are not directly controlled. This results in more subjective means of data collection such as interviews.

The authors of *Dimensions of Thinking* suggest that students can practice these three phases of systematic inquiry through a five step process involving: (1) identification of the problem, (2) recall of relevant information, (3) generating hypotheses, (4) testing of hypotheses, and (5) stating conclusions based on analysis of information collected.

At first glance, the instructional application of research appears impractical in the arts. However, students (and teachers) can use research skills in music settings. Research as a thinking process relies heavily on an understanding of music as a discipline of structured knowledge. The formulation of hypothese can be done through aural as well as graphic/textual modeling. The undergraduate or high school student could approach the rules of counterpoint and harmony of the common practice period through systemic study and inquiry.

Techniques could be borrowed from ethnographic research to help junior high students understand musical creativity by interviewing composers and performers. Experiments in aural perception could be undertaken by elementary children that would involve forming predictions (hypotheses) checked by simple monitored observations.

Composition. Of the eight thinking processes selected for discussion, composition would appear to be the one process most characteristic of the arts. While acknowledging that the composition process can result in a dance, painting, poem, or song, the focus of attention in *Dimensions of Thinking* is on creative writing.

Composition is defined as conceiving and developing a product. While the product certainly differs between individuals, the process involved in its creation has great similarity across styles, periods, and materials. The salient features of the creative writing process have direct correlation to the creation of music.

Past views of the writing process conceived it as a series of linear stages that the creator stepped through toward the completion of a finished product. Current models, however, feature the recursive interaction between and among stages. Flower & Hayes (1981) conceive of the writing process as including planning, translating, and reviewing, all under the control of the writer as monitor.

In the *planning* phase, the writer builds an internal representation of the content to be communicated. This involves cognitive abilities such as generating ideas, structuring information into categories, and setting goals. In the second component, *translating,* the writer's internal ideas and content take the form of visible language and in effect make the abstract (the mind) become concrete (written word). The final component is that of *reviewing* by focusing on the evaluation and revision of what has been created so far.

The writer acts as the monitor of the entire process, deciding when to move between the components of planning, translating, and reviewing. The flow is thus not linear, but "looped" or recursive. It is obvious that an important dimension of this model is that of metacognition where the individual is aware of his or her particular pattern of thought.

Turning to a model of the music composition process, two similarities are evident: (1) the recursive nature of the process and (2) phases or components stressing abstract and concrete representation of ideas. The abstract aspects tend to focus primarily on intuitive or creative qualities while concrete facets focus on rational or critical abilities.

By interviewing professional composers, Bennett (1976, 7) developed a model of the process of musical composition that in many ways parallels models from creative writing (see figure 2).

The germinal idea is the initial phase of musical composition as it provides the inspiration or idea for the work. This first phase is viewed as central to the composing process and involves both external and internal events. Examples of external events include environmental occurrences such as a sunset, another work or art, and improvisation in response to other sounds; while examples of internal events include emotional states of consciousness.

The sketch phase involves the transfer of a germinal idea to a visual and more permanent form, preserving it for later use. Frequently the sketch directly leads to the next phase—the final draft. It is important to note that the process may flow between first draft, sketches, and germinal ideas, leading to additional "first drafts" and thus more new material.

The elaboration and refinement phase involve the working and reworking of germinal ideas. This results in a final draft and copying of the score, which is sometimes followed by a revision phase.

The importance of this optional revision (often made after performance of the work) depends on the composer.

Dichotomies of abstract/concrete representation of musical ideas and intuitive/rational operations are evident in this model. The germinal idea phase is primarily spontaneous and intuitive, while the first draft, elaboration and refinement, and revision phases are significantly more logical and rational.

The fostering of experiences in music composition carries important education considerations. Developing germinal and internal musical ideas relies heavily on long-term memory and past experience. Thus students cannot be expected to compose in a style or medium that is unfamiliar. The metacognitive nature of the entire process suggests that students must be made conscious of the various aspects and operations inherent in producing a creative product. Students will need guidance and practice in monitoring their own creative musical behavior. This means that students must have the opportunity to hear their compositions in both draft and final form. Composition as a thinking process provides learners a means of applying a wide variety of cognitive operations toward musical conceptual and skill areas.

Oral Discourse. Dimensions of Thinking views oral discourse as the process of verbal interaction between two or more people. It is also the only thinking process conceived as encompassing both knowledge acquisition and knowledge production/application.

An important quality of this thinking process is its immediate nature. We do not embark on oral discourse with the intention of yielding a product within an artistic mode. Rather, we improvise and react, shaping our ideas as the commu-

41

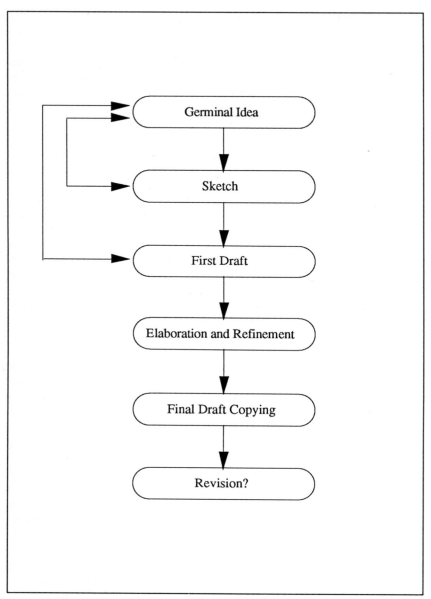

Figure 2. Model of the process of music composition

nication develops. Such discourse involves internal as well as external dialogues and, in fact, internal "self-talk" can be a powerful means of shaping and developing one's knowledge, beliefs, and attitudes.

Oral language has always maintained a strong position in education as a conscious tool for learning and instruction. *Dimensions of Thinking* suggests that oral discourse should be used to develop all other thinking processes and core thinking skills.

> [Oral discourse] is a key pedagogical method because students who make meaning by stating academic knowledge in their own words demonstrate a depth of understanding well beyond what is reflected in recitation or in the recognition-testing of many paper-and-pencil tests. To become conversant with a subject is to have used oral discourse in significant and personal ways (64).

This powerful statement concerning oral discourse—a discourse based on text and spoken word—should also be conceived as including *musical* discourse. Our definition of musical parallels that of oral discourse—the process of musical interaction between two or more people. An example of such interaction could be the sharing of musical ideas via the performance of those ideas. While the purpose of oral language is to communicate, the purpose of music is to express. Students should be able to demonstrate their knowledge of music by the conscious selection and application or oral *and* musical means.

The Content for Thinking Processes in Music

We view music not only as an art-form, but also as the subject area of a curriculum. Throughout the discussion of thinking processes, the awareness and understanding of a content area was conceived as crucial for any further acquisition and application of knowledge. As an example, principles by their very nature describe how concepts are related to one another within the network of a content area. Music is indeed an art-form—one that is a structured discipline as well as a natural part of the human experience.

Any musical activity with an instructional focus or purpose can be described by its content (element or concept), its context (thinking process or musical behavior), and its quality (creative or critical). As an example, students creating rhythmic ostinato accompaniment for a well-known folk song are involved in an experience whose *content* is the concept of rhythm, *context* is the thinking process of composition, and *quality* is intuitive and creative. A junior high clarinet player who monitors and improves his own performance in a rehearsal would be making performance decisions (context) concerning tone quality (content) in a critical manner (quality).

These three characteristics (content, context, and quality) of an instructional musical activity form the basis of a model for musical thinking and curriculum development. While acknowledging that the real world is not organized into such neat three dimensional units, such a view can foster our thinking toward balancing musical experiences within a comprehensive arts curriculum.

Thinking processes are complex and will require time to develop for individual learners. For music education to foster such thinking, curriculum development must *consciously* incorporate and integrate experiences and opportunities for students to use their thinking process effectively.

5

CORE THINKING SKILLS IN MUSIC

JANET R. BARRETT

When students are actively engaged in "doing" music, they experience what it means to act and think like a musician. Our goal as music educators is to provide opportunities for students to experience that transformation that allows them to function not as individuals learning about music, but instead as musicians involved in the performance, description, and creation of music. Skills of performance have long served as the indicator of this transformation—students exhibit musicianly behavior as they *act* as musicians. But what of skills of cognition—indicators that students *think* as musicians?

This chapter will focus on mental operations used to make meaning and to generate new knowledge. These operations, often called thinking skills, have become the rallying cry of those advocating emphasis on the process used to learn in addition to the content learned. This chapter will elaborate on the "relatively specific cognitive operations that can be considered the 'building blocks' of thinking" (Marzano, et al., 147). These core skills are essential for the utilization of other dimensions of cognition including metacognition, thinking processes, and critical and creative thinking.

Selecting a core of thinking skills from the universe of possible cognitive operations was acknowledged by the authors of *Dimensions of Thinking* as a problematic task. They chose a twenty-one thinking skills and grouped in eight categories according to the following criteria: (1) Skills documented in various strands of psychological research or in philosophy as important to learning or thinking; (2) skills appearing to be teachable, as established through research studies, field testing, or widespread use in the classroom; and (3) skills valued by educators as important for students to learn (Marzano et al., 69). The list of skills found in figure 1 is adapted from the summary outline provided by the authors.

I. Skills of Knowledge Acquisition

    A. Focusing Skills—attending to selected pieces of information and ignoring others

        1. *Defining problems:* clarifying needs, discrepancies, or puzzling situations

        2. *Setting goals:* establishing direction and purpose

    B. Information-Gathering Skills—bringing to conciousness the relevant data needed for cognitive processing

        3. *Observing*: obtaining information through one or more senses

        4. *Formulating questions*: seeking new information through inquiry

    C. Remembering Skills—storing and retrieving information

        5. *Encoding*: storing information in long-term memory

        6. *Recalling*: retrieving information from long-term memory

II. Skills of Processing

    A. Organizing Skills—arranging information so it can be used more effectively

        7. *Comparing*: noting similarities and differences between or among entities

---

8. *Classifying*: grouping and labeling entities on the basis of their attributes

9. *Ordering*: sequencing entities according to a given criterion

10. *Representing*: changing the form but not the substance of information

B. Analyzing Skills—clarifying existing information by examining parts and relationships

11. *Identifying attributes and components*: determining characteristics or parts of something

12. *Identifying relationships and patterns*: recognizing ways elements are related

13. *Identifying main ideas:* identifying the central element; for example, the hierarchy of key ideas in a message or line of reasoning

14. *Identifying errors:* recognizing logical fallacies and other mistakes and, where possible, correcting them

III. **Skills of Transfer and Application**

A. Generating Skills

15. *Inferring:* going beyond available information to identify what reasonably may be true

16. *Predicting:* anticipating next events, or the outcome of a situation

17. *Elaborating:* explaining by adding details, examples, or other relevant information

B. Integrating Skills—connecting and combining information

18. *Summarizing*: combining information efficiently into a cohesive statement

19. *Restructuring*: Changing existing knowledge structures to incorporate new information

C Evaluating Skills—assessing the reasonableness and quality of ideas

20. *Establishing criteria*: setting standards for making judgments

21. *Verifying*: confirming the accuracy of claims

Figure 1. Adapted from Dimensions of Thinking *(147–48).*

Relationship of Thinking Skills to Content

Examination of this list raises the question of how these skills relate specifically to music. Are there broad general skills used in any content area in addition to specialized skills found only in certain contexts? We use these operations to think *about* something—musical content. The structure of that content reveals patterns of melody, rhythm, harmony, and form that are perceived by the student. These relationships of sound form a web of content, often referred to as "domain-specific knowledge." This web of content knowledge and thinking skills used to expand and elaborate the web interacts as the learner becomes capable of independent musical thought. In turn, developments of thought are demonstrated in musical behaviors, which become increasingly more refined and necessitate further cycles of content knowledge acquisition served by thinking skills resulting in further action.

Observing musicians in action or reflecting on one's own musical involvement can be useful in inferring the mental processes used to function expressively and thoughtfully. *Performers* use many cognitive skills to realize a pre-existent composition as they sight read a new composition, polish its performance through cycles of rehearsal and practice, and ultimately present an expert rendition.

Describers make musical processing transparent as what is heard is verbalized, shown through movement, or represented graphically. In order to interact with a composition, the describer must purposefully direct attention toward elemental features of the music, identify patterns of sound and relationships among patterns and use those patterns in predicting future events in a composition. For example, an individual might describe movement toward closure or continuation of perceived patterns in terms of an expectation to be resolved.

Creators of music either invent in a continuous flow (improvisation) or preserve the results of inventive activity in a form to be performed later (composition). Either behavior accesses knowledge of stylistic devices in music and elaboration of those devices according to some criteria that can be used as a measure of the music's expressive potential.

Thinking Skills and Instruction

How does an understanding of the thinking skills summarized above translate into application in a music classroom where goals include the thinking and musicianly behaviors just described? Few would argue that many musical cognitive behaviors are acquired by students without the need for formal training or instruction. Kindergarten children enter school with a bank of musical experience and a repertoire of musical sounds that they can accurately predict. Through repeated experience in informal settings, they have already acquired some enactive representations of musical syntax. Building on these informal experiences, formal instruction enables them to label patterns of familiar sounds so that they can name what they already hear. But formal education seeks to move beyond mere labelling to the point at which children can manipulate musical materials to create new relationships and to deepen understandings beyond intuitive graspings.

Teachers observe students as they use thinking skills independently, without prompting or formal tuition. There are occasions, however, when teachers identify difficulties in solving musical problems. At these times, direct instruction in thinking skills to complement musical behaviors might be appropriate. After consideration of student needs, a music educator might select a particular skill for emphasis from the catalog of possible skills, identify a strategy that will assist the execution of that skill, and plan for opportunities in which students might practice and refine their use of the skill. Some of the skills mentioned by the authors of *Dimensions of Thinking* are readily found in music classes and might serve as a starting point for instruction. In the following discussion of pertinent thinking skills, examples will illustrate both independent use by students and specific teacher modeling of instructional strategies to highlight skills in addition to presentation of musical content.

Skills of Knowledge Acquisition

The categories of focusing, information-gathering and remembering skills listed in figure 1 describe skills that assist the learner in directing attention toward the musical context, gleaning information from the source, and storing what has been perceived for subsequent retrieval as needed. One such skill is that of *goal-setting*, as a learner sets expectations for a task to follow. This skill may be evident in individual situations, as a musician establishes goals for a practice session, or modeled in a large-group setting, as a teacher leads the class to identify what is already known (involving remembering), what needs to be explored (through analyzing), and how the group will know when goals are achieved (by evaluating).

A fundamental task of music teachers is the development of acute perceptual abilities requiring the cognitive skill of *observing*. Learners frequently encounter complex musical structures in music examples. Teachers formulate questions and plan strategies to help the learner focus on certain elements of the example within the context of the expressive whole. Although a review of insights regarding perception is beyond the scope of this discussion, it might be helpful to briefly reflect upon the range of examples presented to learners at various stages of ability. Sequencing observations from simple to complex might span a continuum from demands placed on the learner to attend to repeated rhythm patterns found in a short listening example to concentrating on the nuance of phrase when comparing various recordings of a particular string quartet. In addition, the learner's degree of familiarity with the composition will affect quality of the observation. Unfamiliar pieces pose particular demands on processing capabilities of the learner, which are gradually lessened through repeated hearings of the same composition.

In order for learners to build a repertoire of musical examples, a way to "encode" or store the musical information becomes necessary. Teachers assist in this process by representing the musical example with graphics or traditional notation that strengthen the encoding process by paring a visual image of the sound with the sound source. A "picture" of the sound makes it possible for the information to be stored in two forms—as an auditory image and a visual image. Directing learners to describe what is heard through movement also allows for dual forms of storage—auditory and kinesthetic. Rehearsal and mnemonic devices are frequently used as strategies to assist the encoding of meaningful information.

Other knowledge acquisition skills might include *formulating questions* about the content to set up expectations for learning. For example, before listening to a piece, students might ask a series of questions they expect to have answered as they listen. *Recalling* is often triggered by a verbal cue to activate prior knowledge, relating what is already known to a new task confronting the learner.

These skills seem fundamental to the learning process and are often a part of students' and teachers' battery of cognitive skills. They are discussed here, however, to stress the importance of these processes before musicians can engage in other, more complex operations. These skills of knowledge acquisition are central to the establishment of an experiential base in music.

Skills of Processing

Some categories of skills refer to what the learner "does with" the knowledge after it has been acquired—reorganizing the content or identifying relationships within the content that are not explicitly stated. One group of such skills may be categorized as *skills of organization* (see figure 1).

Comparing examples to ascertain similarities and differences illustrates one possible use of an organizing strategy presented by a teacher during instruction. If the musical examples to be compared demonstrate readily perceivable contrasts, students are generally able to articulate clear distinctions between them. If the examples used are more sophisticated, however, a teacher may notice that students have difficulties in going beyond surface features in a comparison task. In this case, the teacher might choose to present a strategy such as the following to stimulate refined comparison: (1) list features of example A; (2) list features of B; (3) rearrange lists so that similar features are adjacent; (4) determine whether differences can be expressed in a parallel fashion; (5) draw a conclusion about the degree of similarity between the two examples and describe as precisely as possible (Stahl 1985). The decision to explicitly present a strategy for use in a thinking task is sometimes appropriate when students have difficulty processing the information without direct instruction. (For further strategies, see Beyer 1987, 1988).

Classifying involves grouping items into categories based on attributes of the items. Early experiences with classification require the learner to recognize easily perceivable differences between a limited number of items to form groups (for example, a tuba and a trumpet are blown to make sound; a drum and a cymbal are struck). As the learner becomes more sophisticated, classification systems become more subtle, requiring finer distinctions. Students might be requested to classify jazz recordings by school or traditions of playing. A crucial step in classifying is the labeling process, which aids the students to recall the item at a later time, along with items belonging to the same category.

Ordering skills allow students to sequence temporal events. Young students might sequence musical events by arranging pictures to correspond with the text and phrase structure in a simple song. With expanded experiences and developing cognitive ability, musical examples of greater length and variable structure may be used. As students gain understanding of musical structure, their ability to recognize and predict common forms such as theme and variations, rondo, and so forth, assists them in ordering the events heard in unfamiliar compositions.

Representing musical ideas by changing the form but not the substance of the information often serves as a check for comprehension as well as a means of clarifying meaning. For example, a student having trouble explaining how a particular passage should be phrased might be asked to demonstrate the phrasing vocally or instrumentally. Asking "What is another way you can tell me or show me your idea?" encourages students to share information in a variety of representations and provides the teacher with visible evidence of understanding. In addition, teachers may use a battery of examples, analogies, or diagrams to represent fundamental ideas in various forms, thus helping students realize that ideas may be represented in diverse ways.

Recalling our formal musical training highlights the importance of the skills of analysis. (See figure 1.) Analysis challenges the learner to *identify attributes and components,* recognizing that a whole may be made up of parts. This attention to the features of a piece is also crucial to the process of concept formation, for example, what constitutes or does not constitute an example of a musical style based on the attributes present in the music.

Identifying relationships and patterns is central to uncovering the underlying structure of a composition, which can aid in memorization for performance, depth in description, and as an impetus for creating new works with similar structures. It is often wise to identify these relationships through discussion so that able learners are reinforced in their thoughts and less able learners are provided with a framework for enhanced understanding. Skillful teachers search for instructional strategies and musical materials that will exemplify relationships and assist the learner by "sharing" analysis to eventual independent consideration of possible interactions among musical elements.

Identifying main ideas, while most frequently referred to as a strategy for understanding in a written context, might be applied to music as a student picks out the primary themes or motives used in a composition. To completely grasp the meaning of the work, the learner must also recognize transformations of these musical ideas as various compositional devices are used as the composition unfolds.

Finally, *identifying errors* is fundamental to the cycle of rehearsal and performance mentioned in the previous section. One strategy for helping students in a class or rehearsal situation learn to identify their own performance errors might be to listen to an audiotape of a work "in progress" in order to offer suggestions of corrections and alterations that would lead towards a more musically satisfying performance.

Skills of Transfer and Application

Transfer and application skills are necessary if the learner is to draw on principles or generalizations to bridge from a known context to a new one. In this sense, the learner makes new connections by relating what is understood from past or present experiences to unfamiliar events and experiences. Sometimes this bridging takes dramatic form when a learner recognizes a familiar relationship in a new context and responds with an "Aha!" Sometimes the instance of transfer is more gradual as new learning is blended with previous understandings over time, such as in the preparation of a piece for performance that spans several months of rehearsal. Categories of skills included in this group include generating, integrating and evaluating skills.

Inferring, one type of generating skill, involves "going beyond available information to identify what reasonably may be true" (Marzano et al., 148). Teachers can encourage students to infer by setting up problems posed in the form of a hypothesis, an "if, then" relationship. For example, a question posed as a hypothesis might prompt the transfer of common knowledge from one musical behavior, such as listening, to another behavior such as composing: "If Mozart altered the A section significantly the last time it was repeated to establish a feeling of finality, then what might be appropriate decisions for you to make when completing your composition to achieve the same musical goal?" Students can be challenged to develop similar questions to predict performance decisions, to describe common relationships or to compose a work based on a suggested model.

Predicting future aural events in a musical setting requires that students compare what has just been heard to a storehouse of remembered musical examples in order to form an educated guess as to what is yet to come. An instructional strategy to promote the use of this thinking skill was mentioned as part of a framework for musical comprehension in the preceding chapter on thinking processes. Students might, for example, preview the score of a work to be heard, recall pertinent information from memory, and construct a hypothesis defining what they expect to hear. While listening to the work, students check for confirmation or rejection of their hypotheses. Challenges of directed listening such as this one often motivate the students to examine the musical example with heightened awareness and to gain a personal sense of accomplishment and satisfaction when predictions are confirmed. As the framework suggests, discussion, confirmation, or rejection of predictions *after* listening often allows students to reflect on the basis for their predictions and to identify gaps in knowledge that might be addressed in subsequent hearings of a composition. Students might also survey a score before performing it for the first time to predict potential problems such as challenging passages or unexpected changes in tempo, texture, and rhythmic pattern.

Elaboration is a useful instructional tool for the teacher and a valuable learning process for the students as new explanations of a phenomenon are created. The use of comparisons, analogies, and metaphors boosts comprehension and retention. In problem-solving situations, representing the problem in an alternate form, such as an analogy, often suggests new strategies or solutions to the learner. Skilled teachers have a repertoire of analogies to draw upon to relate the familiar to the unfamiliar when explaining new or complex content.

For example, they may liken the "pull" of the pitch serving as the tonal center to the pull of a magnet. In addition to using elaboration verbally to clarify understanding, elaboration through manipulation of musical ideas is essential to creative endeavors as a student grapples with the task of embellishing a given melody.

Summarizing is useful when forming a generalization that can then be applied in a broader context. Students might notice that the repetition of a pattern in the example being studied sets up certain expectations that are only made apparent when a change occurs in the music. The teacher might help students summarize their observations by asking, "How could we state this idea in such a way that it might apply to examples other than the one we are now hearing?" A statement could be constructed by students using terms that have generalizable power: "When a repeated musical patterns is eventually changed in some way, the change becomes highlighted for the listener." Further examples should then be examined to test the generalizability of the statement to see if it will apply in a variety of contexts.

The need for *restructuring* is encountered as the situations require that students significantly shift perspective or systems of categorization in conceptual structures. Hearing a different work representative of a particular style may, for example, require that the learner alter existing knowledge structures in order to incorporate new information. Since this process is highly dependent upon the learner's existing conceptual framework and the naive conceptions (or misconceptions) the learner might hold, it may not be readily apparent to the teacher that the student is involved, or needs to be involved, in restructuring existing knowledge. However, occasionally "glitches" in understanding, such as when a student is asked about the dynamic level of a piece and responds by describing the tempo, may signal a need to reorganize or restructure thought regarding a particular area. When a student seemingly "runs into a brick wall" a teacher might assist the student to explore alternative ways of looking at the musical problem.

Establishing criteria suggests that the learner evaluate a composition, performance, or description (their own or others) by using a given set of standards or by developing a new set. Developing such criteria often requires consideration of the weight or relative importance of various factors. Students can be encouraged to make evaluative statements about musical materials, performances, discussions and the like in light of standards agreed upon by the group. As students explain why they have made a particular judgment, the criteria for that judgment should be clearly stated. If omitted, the teacher should prompt students to articulate the reasoning supporting a given judgment.

Verifying is defined as "confirming the accuracy of claims." As suggested earlier, students might confirm the accuracy or aptness of predictions after listening to or performing an unfamiliar composition. Students might also engage in verification as they test the generalizations they have devised when involved in summarizing observations. For example, if students have generalized that composers of program music frequently use accelerandi to increase the feeling of tension in a story told through music, they might search for additional examples to verify their idea as well as examples that might lead them to modify their generalizations.

Implications for Instruction

Students often demonstrate their use of thinking skills through the overt behaviors they exhibit in class as they articulate a line of reasoning, ask a perceptive question as they seek to establish connections with material presented in a previous class, or demonstrate their understanding of musical structure through performance. In planning instruction teachers will be sensitive to occasions when such skills are apparently inadequate or underdeveloped. Such observations should be the time for deciding to actively plan to teach the thinking skill in question. Sometimes introduction of a particular strategy for thinking will be necessary for students who do not generate strategies on their own. Articulating the process will serve to strengthen that process and make more likely the possibility that the learner will use these tools when faced with similar problems in the future. One caveat is needed: when identifying and selecting skills for specific focus, limit the number of skills to a small number—two or three perhaps—so that students will have repeated and intense practice in applying these skills in a variety of contexts. Skills will be more likely to transfer if they have been thoughtfully introduced and practiced, in contrast to a "one shot inoculation" of thinking skills instruction.

Music teachers are especially skilled at modeling behaviors that allow students to learn by example. In performance learning situations teachers model everything from the correct pitch and rhythm to the expressive "shaping" of a phrase. Students also learn as teachers model appropriate thinking behaviors. As students listen to teachers "think aloud" they have a chance to view evident examples of thinking processes as well as products of thought. In our discussions we can focus attention on perceptible elements, make links to prior knowledge and explore how musical examples are related in terms of deep principles as well as surface features. Listening to a teacher or another student talk through a problem situation can assure other students that it is common to have difficulties in thinking but that reflective thinkers use thinking skills to work through these difficulties rather than just giving up.

Music classroom environments supportive of thinking skills instruction can be identified if an observer looks for certain characteristics: In such an environment there is a forum for alternate ideas that demonstrates the valuing of diversity rather than conformity of thought; teachers provide "wait time" after asking questions so students have opportunity to formulate reflective responses. Musical materials are chosen carefully to juxtapose situations that invite analysis, transfer, and evaluation. Students are prompted to articulate their thought processes by being asked such questions as, "How did you arrive at that idea?" "What made you think of that?" The dynamic process of discovering musical relationships in such an environment will promote the use of thinking skills and give students the chance to engage in active learning.

Teachers can plan and execute lessons that make it likely that students will acquire musical knowledge, process and shape that knowledge into new conceptual structures, and use those structures when faced with challenges in new learning situations. The thinking skills used by students in the examples cited above are also fundamental to the dispositions of critical and creative thinking and to metacognition. Consideration of the types of skills used and the ways in which teachers can promote their use will contribute to the goal of musical independence in all students.

6

MUSICAL THINKING AND THE YOUNG CHILD

BARBARA ALVAREZ

The thinking processes of the young child are varied, intuitive, and highly imaginative. In the first seven years of life, music and the other arts are natural modes for individual expressiveness and provide many excellent opportunities for exploration. Through creative play, the young child's thinking skills begin to grow and, although some of their musical thinking skills are based on verbal experiences, the majority are evidenced in a variety of nonverbal, sensory experiences. In order to nurture musical cognition in the early years, teachers need to think holistically. Cognitive development intertwines with the child's growth of attitudes, skills, and knowledge.

The link between the young child's musical experiences and the development of thinking skills is clearly within this view of total development. Fifty years ago many early childhood programs were based primarily on affective goals. Today, with the realization of the importance of the early years in development, many programs are emphasizing cognitive, labeling goals. However, early experiences that emphasize *only* cognitive goals run the risk of expecting children to grapple with knowledge they can cope with intellectually but not emotionally or physically.

> Intelligence requires not just the use of the rational, analytic thinking function, but also the spatial, holistic processes of the brain, and the integration of the emotional physical sensing, and intuitive thinking functions as well. While these functions can be regarded separately, it is their integration that creates high levels of intelligence and the optimal development of human potential (Clark 1986, 14).

The goal of early childhood development and education must be developmentally appropriate affective, cognitive, and psychomotor growth that will lead toward emotional and intellectual balance. Even a chapter such as this, which focuses on various dimensions of thinking skills means nothing unless one keeps in mind that cognitive goals are but a single integral facet of a holistic approach to child development. This chapter will address the relationships between the dimensions of thinking and the young child's musical thinking, and suggest criteria for developing appropriate learning strategies for three- to seven-year-old children.

The Building Blocks of Musical Thinking

Extensive research into early childhood development has shown just how crucial the early years are in a person's total development. The first seven years of life are thought of as preparatory because the base for all future learning, growth and development is set in those years. The first cognitive growth occurs in nonverbal modes as the young child begins life totally dependent on action and sensory stimulation to perceive and process information. Progress toward logical thought occurs through concrete, literal experiences that begin in sensory-based modes.

The development of the three- to seven-year-old has been mapped out in Piaget's descriptions of the preoperational stage of development. Based on the accomplishments of the infant and toddler in the sensorimotor stage, the three-year-old "is already a more competent problem solver than the adult members of any other animal species on earth (Hohmann, Banet, and Weikart 1979, 4).

The preschooler's problem solving skills reflect the ability to think about actions in everyday experiences without solving every problem through a physical, trial and error method. Preoperational thought is characterized by egocentrism and ideas are understood only in light of the child's own experiences and viewpoints. The symbolic function is developing although the imaginative world of the child is often intermixed with the reality of symbols and what they represent. An important factor in the young child's thinking process is the lack of reversible thought in considering relationships in a sequence. The mental structure does not yet allow the child to mentally transform or reverse sequences. For example, numbering songs such as "The Twelve Days of Christmas" and "Ten Little Indians" work beautifully when you count forward and fail miserably when you count backward!

Just as all skills in the early childhood years are building blocks for later learning and development, so the first music thinking skills are the base for future involvement with music. Sensory, action-based musical experiences can allow children to begin to use their own ideas in making sense of music and this is the beginning of musical thinking.

There are a number of ways that young children can participate in musical experiences with optimum opportunities for the development of music thinking skills. All of these opportunities relate in some way to the way children "work" during a process adults label "play." Opinions about the value of play have changed over the years but today there is increasing support for this important part of being a child (Frost 1985).

As children participate in free-play activities they are in charge of their own actions and so undoubtedly are using thinking skills as they go about their "work" deciding "what," "how," and "why." In addition to providing an abundant amount of such "free play," adults can encourage and enhance musical thinking skills both directly and indirectly.

Implications of *Dimensions of Thinking* for the Young Child

The applicability of the various "dimensions of thinking" to musical experiences has been discussed in preceding chapters. Metacognition, critical and creative thinking, the thinking processes and the core thinking skills are the main topics used in this summary of thinking in the classroom. How can such a theoretical framework be applied in early childhood music experiences? The most applicable skills, pertinent in any early childhood program, are the *core thinking skills* which have been referred to as the "building blocks" of thinking (Marzano et al. 1988, 147). This category includes the acts of focusing, information-gathering, remembering, organizing, analyzing, generating, integrating, and evaluating. The more complex *thinking processes* such as concept formation, problem solving, research, and composition are complex sequences that are enhanced by a firm foundation in the core thinking skills.

Metacognition in musical experiences involves the awareness of one's performing, listening and creating skills. The enhancement of metacognitive skills can be a thread throughout musical experiences in the early years as teachers encourage children to think about how they performed certain activities, what they would change or keep the same about these musical decisions, and even why a certain experience had been chosen. A teacher performing musically with even the simplest classroom instruments can attend to the control of the sound's tone color, dynamic level, or tempo, while modeling musical expressiveness. Young children will begin to copy these behaviors and begin to think about qualifying the sounds they make. When this happens the process of metacognition is under way.

Creative thinking is an integral part of the role playing that takes place in the early childhood play environment. Therefore, this period of growth is a prime time for the early development of creative thinking skills. While the core thinking skills are specific cognitive functions that are usually developed through direct instruction, creative thinking, which takes place during free play, can be a way of observing how children go about thinking. A parent coping with a three-year-old who is walking about with a stick in hand striking every object in the environment three times (including the kitty cat!) might well tell the child, "Stop that!" A teacher striving for the development of creative thinking would, after taking care of the cat, notice that the child is listening with delight and might join in with the game, beginning to identify her favorite sounds. Soon several children might be involved and you may hear them saying, "Listen to this! This is my favorite!" Creative thinking would be taking place.

Critical thinking tends to involve more objective, logical thinking processes. Since young children have not yet developed concrete or formal operations, as described by Piaget, much of the direct programmatic instruction that might be appropriate later is totally inappropriate at this time. Most vital are early experiences with creative thinking and the core thinking skills if children are to profit from later experiences in logical, critical thinking that the upper elementary schools seek to provide.

Strategies for Developing Thinking Skills in the Young Child

Following are several strategies that suggest ways that the various dimensions of thinking can be nurtured in early childhood musical experiences. Sample Strategy 1 (figure 1) explores the enhancement of core thinking skills and creative thinking skills in a preschool play setting. The teacher models ways to explore singing versus speaking with puppets and children continue the exploration in their own play settings. Sample Strategy 2 (figure 2) uses direct instruction to encourage the use of four core thinking skills. The incorporation of students ideas and responsibility for thinking is the key to enhancing thinking skills in a typical rhyme procedure such as the one described in this strategy. Sample Strategy 3 (figure 3) is also an example of direct instruction. The children are practicing many of the same core thinking skills as in Strategy 2, but their responsibility for analyzing and generating new information is taken a step further.

Criteria for Developing Strategies

The examples of teaching strategies provided in Figures 1 through 3 use direct and indirect instruction to tap the young child's world of play in order to enhance the development of thinking skills. Teachers need to be able to design many such strategies on a daily basis. The following criteria need to be considered when planning strategies to help enhance young children's musical skills.

1. Design each experience with consideration for the total development development of the child.
2. Because young children are still very egocentric in their functioning, give children the opportunity to make choices.
3. Because play is a young child's work, and play is more process than product-oriented, strive to incorporate a play atmosphere even in direct instruction musical experiences.
4. Provide ample opportunity for physical and kinesthetic involvement since the child's thinking is based on action.
5. Remember that the child's thinking is highly imaginative. The use of imagery in instructional settings can enhance the young child's motivation to explore and think.
6. Stress indirect teaching. The learning environments of young children should be rich with enticing stimuli and encouraging adults.
7. Because young children generally focus on one new aspect of an experience at a time, include known skills and knowledge with the one new aspect that the children can explore.
8. Include new experiences in which known skills and knowledge can be practiced through repetition.
9. Use developmental labels only as guidelines for developing strategies. Some children are probably "ahead" in some characteristics and "behind" in others.
10. Play must always precede the understanding and use of various thinking skills. We "do" and then we can "understand."

The young child lives in a world of imagination and possibilities. Through observations of effective modeling and active participation in a rich musical environment, children can direct their own musical learning and achieve a balance between skills, attitudes and knowledge. By helping young children to refine their thinking skills we can hope for greater success in their future musical endeavors as they continue to perform, listen, and create.

Sample Strategy 1

Materials: Collection of hand puppets, finger puppets, or puppets on sticks

Age level: Ages 3 and 4

Procedure:

Initial Activity

Enhancement of *Core Thinking Skills*—focusing, information gathering, organizing, and analyzing

During free play time, the teacher gathers a variety of hand puppets and puppets on sticks and sits with them in a free area of the preschool. As children show interest, she begins to ask individual puppets if they are feeling like singing or speaking today. With puppets who "say" they want to speak, a known rhyme is recited and the teacher and children join in speaking the rhyme. With puppets who "say" they want to sing, the teacher and children sing a known song with the puppet.

The teacher helps children identify the characteristics of singing versus speaking. The children close their eyes and identify singing and speaking examples from puppets, other children, or the teacher.

The teacher then discovers a special puppet who wants to sing *and* speak. Another song is sung; another rhyme is spoken. The teacher (or perhaps the last puppet) begins to ask individual children if they would like to sing or speak, and more examples are sung or spoken. The puppets are left out in the free-play area and the children are encouraged to continue exploring both singing and speaking on their own.

Development

Enhancement of *Creative Thinking Skills*

Enhancement of *Core Thinking Skills*—generating

The exploration of singing and speaking becomes a theme for the day in all play areas, encouraged by teachers and aides. The teacher directly or indirectly helps those students who still need assistance in "finding" their singing voices. As the school day ends, children are encouraged to try the "game" at home and see if family members can guess whether they are singing or speaking.

Figure 1. Indirect instruction

Sample Strategy 2

Enhancement of Core Thinking Skills—focusing, information gathering, remembering, organizing

Materials: Copy of the rhyme, "Wee Willie Winkie:"

Wee Willie Winkie runs through the town,
Upstairs and downstairs in his nightgown.
Rapping at the windows, crying through the locks,
"Are the children in their beds, for now it's eight o' clock!"

Pictures:

Age level: Ages 5 and 6

Procedure:

Speak the rhyme with heightened inflection. Have the children identify the little boy's name and what he's doing in the rhyme. Discuss and act out unclear passages.

Speak the rhyme again. Stop at the end of each phrase and ask children for ideas of finger movements to illustrate the rhyme. Have children join in the speaking of the rhyme, adding the finger movements. Try this at varying tempos and dynamic levels chosen by the children.

Show the children the four pictures (not in order). Speak the rhyme and have children figure out the correct order of the pictures. Discuss. Put the pictures in order and speak the rhyme again.

Dramatize the rhyme. Perform the rhyme like a silent movie—act it out while thinking the words.

Put together a "final performance" from the various activities explored. Add an introduction or coda. Help children select the steps, and then perform them without stopping.

Figure 2. Direct instruction

Sample Strategy 3

Materials: Song—"Simon Says"

Si-mon says, "Touch your eyes."___   Si-mon says, "Touch your nose."___

Touch your ears,   Touch your head,   Si-mon says, "Touch your toes."___

Age level: Ages 5–7.

Procedure:

Initial Activity—focusing, information gathering, remembering, organizing

Remind the children of the rules of "Simon Says" and play a bit of the game. Sing the new song and have the children play the game. (Don't do the action unless Simon says!)

Sing the song at different tempi until the children have heard and participated in the song several times. Ask the children to identify how many commands are in the song and how many are "Simon says" commands (five; three).

Sing the song again and visually chart the commands as they are sung by drawing a series of lines: _____ _____ _____ _____ _____

Identify which lines indicate "Simon says" commands. Have everyone sing the whole song and do the actions.

Development—analyzing, generating

Ask the children how the song could be changed each time to make it into a more challenging game. (Change "eyes," "nose," and so on.) Ask what will be easier about playing the game with this song than with the real "Simon Says" game. (The "Simon says" commands will always be in the same place in the song.)

Sing the song with new words as the children follow. Ask for volunteers to be the leader and to sing the song each time with new words.

Ask the children how the song could be made as hard as the real game. Singing only on "sol" and "mi," improvise a new melody and commands with and without the words, "Simon says." For example, you could sing:

Touch your head.   Si-mon says, "Touch your head."___

Improvise a variety of melodies and commands.

When the children are ready (probably not on the first day), ask for volunteers to be the leader and improvise a melody and words.

Figure 3. Direct instruction

7

MUSICAL THINKING IN THE GENERAL MUSIC CLASSROOM

MARY P. PAUTZ

The elementary general music teacher can certainly empathize with the White Rabbit, watch in hand, as he scurried nervously in many directions. One of the greatest sources of stress in an elementary general music teacher's life is time or, rather, the lack of it. Simply being able to find time to help students acquire the musical concepts and experiences I as a music teacher consider essential creates a feeling of fighting the clock. But this self-imposed problem is compounded by the demands of the principal and parents who expect holiday and seasonal programs as well as by the faculty's requests to have music correlated with everything from dental health to sex education. Further compounding the sense of frustration is the complaint from the middle school music teacher that the elementary music teacher "has had the kids for six years and hasn't taught them anything!" "And now they tell me I'm supposed to teach students to think?"

What is an elementary general music teacher to do? How is the precious amount of time for music to be used? What kind of planning needs to take place? What implications do the theories proposed in *Dimensions of Thinking* have to do with planning for elementary general music? If music teachers do not have adequate time now to present the musical concepts and experiences considered essential, is it reasonable to expect attention and time devoted to the teaching of core thinking skills, critical and creative thinking processes, and metacognition? ("I'm late! I'm late! For a very important date!")

Before one can decide how to use the time, how to plan, and how, if at all, to incorporate the teaching of thinking into the elementary music class one must first review, and perhaps redefine, the goals of elementary general music. A nebulous goal such as "to love music" or "to enjoy music class" will need to be replaced by a specific, measurable and attainable goal: to produce independent musicians. Other goal statements such as to sing in tune or to read music notation will be recognized as objectives supportive of that primary goal, rather than as separate goals.

Once the goal, to produce independent musicians, is accepted as the primary goal, planning becomes a process for finding the answer to the question, "What must I, as an elementary music teacher, do to help children become independent musicians? What performance skills do they need? What cognitive skills do they need?" The second question is as important as the first for to know *how a musician thinks* is as vital as to know *how a musician performs*. Consequently, both types of skills must be included in the musical education of children. As we plan, we must devise strategies to help children learn to think as carefully as we plan ways to help them learn to sing in tune.

In order for this to happen, we must have a dual agenda that will include helping children develop a rich base of musical knowledge and skills while providing them with a repertoire of cognitive and metacognitive skills and strategies that will enable them to use that knowledge and skill efficiently in meaningful contexts. Education is a process of generating relationships. It is not enough to have students acquire a set body of musical skills and knowledge; they must be able to create new knowledge and expand their skills! Only then can our goal of helping students become intellectually and creatively independent be said to be achieved. Not only must students be culturally literate, they must be culturally thoughtful.

When the relationship of elementary music to the dimensions of thinking, two traditional sayings come to mind, each with its parallel in music teaching:

Give a person a fish and he will not be hungry for a day; teach him how to fish and he will not be hungry for a lifetime.

Teach a child a song by rote and he can sing that song until he tires of it; teach a child strategies to think about and to read music and he can enjoy a lifetime of songs.

For those who only have a hammer, all problems are viewed as nails.

Restrict a child's understanding to rock music and he must evaluate all music using only the standards of rock music.

Two more sayings also serve to express the impact of the dimensions of thinking on elementary education:

Give a child the strategies and experiences to explore many kinds of music and he or she can choose from a vast array of music.

Restrict a child to being a passive receiver of information and the child will know only that which has been taught; give a child cognitive and metacognitive tools and he or she will generate knowledge and music which does not even exist today.

In an effort to achieve as much as possible in the shortest amount of time, we often find ourselves trying to save time by giving children information rather than setting up opportunities for discovery learning. It can prove to be a costly saving when children leave sixth grade knowing a certain repertoire of songs and patterns but unable to proceed independently to learn other music. ("I'm late! I'm late! For a very important date!") Students must be encouraged, expected, and required to *discover* musical knowledge every time they are in music class, for out of the discovering they will come to *value* music, to understand it and to gain skill in performing, describing or creating it. As elementary general music teachers we need to understand and come to terms with the fact that thinking takes time, that creating takes time, and that enabling students to become independent learners takes time. As a teacher, one cannot be content just to keep students busy and involved (so they won't have time to get into trouble); one must be concerned as to whether the involvement is really musical or thoughtful.

One must also constantly keep in mind that good teaching does not mean making a lesson so clear that students do not have to think. If I continue to teach by rote when students are ready for graphic representation, am I using that precious amount of time well? Am I truly teaching or simply entertaining if I continue to use material that students can do comfortably and never edge them into a more difficult level? On the other hand, am I teaching if I rush them into symbols and kid myself into thinking that they are reading those symbols, when all they are really doing is listening to a recording and learning by rote as meaningless notes blur on the page in front of them? ("I'm late! I'm late! For a very important date!")

What frame of mind do we need if we are to be effective teachers? We need to realize that to be a teacher is to be a facilitator, a guide, a nurturer of curiosity, a cognitive referee rather than a teller, an expert, a disseminator of knowledge. We need to realize that to be a teacher is to be a lifelong learner ourselves, that to teach is to learn along with the students. We must encourage students to join us in becoming mental explorers and strategic thinkers.

As teachers we need to be willing to share the responsibility for learning with our students. We need to reward good thinking as much as the correct answer; we need to create an environment that encourages risk-taking as well as skill acquisition. We need to help students to become persistent, to work beyond their limits, to be aware of resources, to learn from failure. Such a frame of mind must begin with the planning process.

Regardless of whether one views the writing of lesson plans as a necessary evil or as an indispensable tool, few teachers make no plans at all. The process engaged in and the final written product, however, will vary from teacher to teacher, as illustrated in these examples:

Teacher number one begins to thumb through the music book and finds "The Battle Hymn of the Republic." The teacher down page number, looks over the song and decides to focus on dotted rhythms. He looks for other patriotic songs with dotted rhythms, and finds "America" and "America the Beautiful." He then prepares a lesson plan. (See figure 1.)

For some teachers, such as the one just described, the planning is complete when the songs and/or listening lessons are chosen. The written plan fits neatly into the typical Lesson Plan Book partitioned into 1"x 1" squares. Certainly selection of the music to be used is one part of the process, but if planning ends there, much will have been left to chance.

Teacher two decides that she wants to continue the study of expression in music. She decides to use the theme of patriotism, looks through book for possible patriotic songs that could be used and finds "The Battle Hymn of the Republic." She decides to call attention to the use of dotted rhythm in this song and other patriotic songs: "The Star Spangled Banner," "America The Beautiful," "God Bless America," and "America." She decides to follow up with Ives' "Variations on America" and writes out her lesson plan. (See figure 2.)

For other teachers, planning will also include identifying the concepts to be learned while studying the chosen materials as well as choosing appropriate activities and preparing appropriate visual or manipulatable materials. This is frequently the model for planning presented in undergraduate music education methods classes. To consciously incorporate the dimensions of thinking into the music-learning process, however, one also needs to plan the sequence of the lesson and the problem-solving strategies the children will be guided to use as the lesson unfolds. Such planning will also involve "scripting" the actual questions to be asked or instructions to be given as demonstrated in the following plan.

Teacher number three also decides that she wants to continue the study of expression in music and also decides to use the theme of patriotism. She looks through book for possible patriotic songs that could be used and finds "The Battle Hymn of the Republic." She brainstorms and comes up with her plan. (See figure 3.)

The plan developed by Teacher number three recognizes that moving toward musical independence is indeed a dual task, requiring musical knowledge and skill as well as cognitive skill. The questions devised by this teacher indicate that there will be an opportunity for more than fact recall. Students will be challenged to use knowledge of all of the elements of music in order to successfully compare arrangements. By working in small groups each student will be measuring the acuity of one's own listening skills with those in the group. By having an opportunity to challenge answers of other groups, they will be involved in analyzing, evaluating and verifying. When answering bonus questions, they will be using generative skills of prediction and inference. Students who participate in this type of class are active participants in the learning process. In addition to learning musical knowledge, they are becoming astute thinkers and critics of musical performance. They will come to music class expecting that this is what one does in music: listen, think, interact, make decisions, make music, and evaluate performances!

The first reaction of some teachers, after reading this third type of lesson planning, may well to say, "I don't have time to write out plans in that detail! I teach forty periods a day!" ("I'm late! I'm late! For a very important date!") Can we afford not to take the time?" To do less is to deny children the opportunity to work with a master teacher! Just as it took time to develop the skills of sight-reading or playing an instrument, so it takes time to develop the skill of developing lesson plans. Just as "practice makes perfect" in the achievement of musical skills, so it is with planning skills. As with the musical skills music teachers already possess, in time, the planning process will become second nature and ideas for plans begin to flow in "script form." Planning for thinking becomes as second nature as choosing quality music and sequencing concepts!

One way to practice planning until it becomes smooth and easy is to use a set of questions as a guide, such as the following. As a teacher brainstorms a plan, this or a similar series may be helpful:

1. On what area of musical concepts should I focus?
2. What specific aspect of the general concept area do I want students to learn?
3. What do the children know already that I can help them build on?
4. What songs have we learned that I could relate to this?
5. How can I make this lesson a problem to be solved? How can I organize it so students will have to think? Can I think of a way that the children can create a similar composition?
6. What help do they need? Instead of telling, what could I do? How could I encourage them to be more actively involved?
7. How can I challenge them? If I ask [a specific question] what might their answers be?
8. What piece of music could I use to make sure they transfer information?
9. What can I ask them to compare or to predict?
10. Shoud I ask them if they can see any patterns?
11. I must remember to ask for the student's thinking process when the answer is incorrect.
12. Is this expecting too much? Can I get this done in thirty minutes, or do I need to plan to take two periods?
13. Do I have a smooth flow from the introduction to the "Developing" section?
14. Is there a better example to use?
15. How have I taught this in previous years?

By asking such questions, the teacher ensures that students will be expanding musical knowledge and skills while building upon the dimensions of thinking in two ways: (1) *As a thinker* when planning lessons, he or she monitors her progress, brainstorms ways of creating musical problems for the students, plans specific questions, and develops problems to be discovered and solved. (2) *As a teacher,* he or she helps students develop strategies as he thinks aloud with them, shares solutions, shapes the flow of the class. In addition to selecting quality music and developing a sequential, conceptually based program, the teacher will provide opportunity for growth in critical and creative thinking. He or she will help students monitor their progress with metacognitive strategies and will provide practice in core thinking skills.

A general music teacher has an awesome responsibility. He or she may be the only music teacher a child knows. He or she has the ability to spark a love of music that will last a lifetime. The ultimate goal must be to help children discover the joy of music, develop the knowledge, the skills, and the values that will enable them to be lifetime lovers and independent learners of music. A music teacher has the wonderful opportunity to help produce the performers, the describers, and the creators of music who are independent because they have learned to use appropriate cognitive skills, to solve musical problems, to monitor their own thinking—and he or she can do that in an amazingly short amount of time *without being late!*

Lesson Plan
"The Battle Hymn of the Republic"—page 34.
Dotted Rhythm

Figure 1. Lesson Plan 1

Lesson Plan

Concept: Expression
Music: "The Battle Hymn of the Republic," "The Star Spangled Banner," "America The Beautiful," "America," "Variations on America" (Ives).
Materials: Charts showing dotted rhythms in icons and notes
Strategy: Point out use of dotted rhythm. Sing other patriotic songs that have dotted rhythm. Call attention to that fact. Discuss how patriotic mood is enhanced by the uneven rhythm. Listen to "Variations on America." Discuss mood of the piece.

Figure 2. Lesson Plan 2

Lesson Plan

Concept: *Expression:* Musical elements are combined into a musical whole to express a musical or extramusical idea.
Music: "The Battle Hymn of Republic," (other examples suggested by class)
Materials: Pictures of robots.
Recordings: Two versions of "The Battle Hymn of the Republic," one by Pete Fountain and one by the Mormon Tabernacle Choir, *Holt Music,* Record V-2

Continued on page 72

Continued on page 72

Figure 3. Lesson Plan 3[1]

---

1. Adapted from E. Meske, B. Andress, M. Pautz, and F. Willman. 1988. *Holt Music.* Grade V (34–35). New York: Holt, Rinehart and Winston.

Lesson Plan, continued

Introducing the lesson: Show pictures of robots. Ask the students to imagine how music performed by robots would sound; how would it be different from that created by human beings? Ask them what decisions humans make each time they sing a song? Invite class to choose a song they learned during the year and make decisions about how it should be performed. Ask if they're satisfied or would they like to make changes. Try several different suggestions; compare and evaluate them.

Developing the lesson:

1. Arrangers also make decisions about how to make the recording interesting. Ask students to pretend they are arranging "The Battle Hymn of the Republic." What decisions would they make?

2. Divide the class into teams of four. Explain that they will hear two arrangements of "Battle Hymn." They are to appoint a scribe who will have a sheet of paper with two columns: one marked "same" and one marked "different." The scribe will write down whatever the group determines was the same decision made by both arrangers or performers (for example, both pieces start softly and then get louder) and what the group decides was different (instrumentation, voices, and so on). Play an arrangement by Pete Fountain and another by the Mormon Tabernacle Choir. Encourage team members to discuss and compare.

3. Explain the scoring system to be used: The first team will give one reason from their "same" column. If all seven groups have the answer, each team receives 100 points. If six groups have the answer, they receive 200 points; if 5 groups are correct, they each receive 300 points and so on. If only one team has the answer, that group wins 700 points! Explain that a team may challenge an answer if they don't agree. At the conclusion of sharing, the two pieces will be replayed and the challenges decided.

4. Ask each group to share answers from the "same" column. Tally points.

5. Ask each group to share answers from the "different" column. Tally points.

6. Offer an opportunity for a bonus question; each group is to complete one of the following statements: "If a rock band were making an arrangement of the song they might...." or, "If, instead of arranging 'The Battle Hymn of the Republic', the groups arranged 'Jingle Bells'...."

Closing the Lesson:

Ask the students to open their books to page 34. Invite the class to listen to a third arrangement noting the effect that the harmonizing part has on the expressiveness of the arrangement. Encourage class to make decisions regarding their own singing of the song. Which ideas will they borrow from Pete Fountain, and which will they borrow from the Mormon Tabernacle Choir?

8

MUSICAL THINKING IN THE CHORAL REHEARSAL

HILARY APFELSTADT

"Monkey see, monkey do."

"Simon says...."

"Stimulus-response"

What do these verbal fragments have in common, and what do they have to do with critical thinking in music? In each phrase there is an implied immediacy; something happens, and almost on impact, so to speak, someone or something responds. How much of our choral rehearsal time is spent on this kind of exchange? "Altos, that's a G not a B. Sing it right this time!" "Basses, raise that top pitch; you're reaching for it instead of singing it dead center." "No—too loud; let's try it again, softer this time." Unfortunately, for most of us, these kinds of directives constitute the bulk of our rehearsal time.

Under the demands of public performance pressures, we seek the most efficient means of getting the music learned, or so we think. In the short term, our students may fix the errors and produce an accurate performance in a relatively brief time. As for the long-term effects, however, we cannot be sure that the "quick fix" will have any lasting impact. The real test is whether the students can apply those learnings to new contexts or whether we must start all over again each time we introduce a new piece of music.

The kind of rote responses alluded to above do have their place in the choral rehearsal; there are times, as in drill and practice sessions, for example, when the teacher's specific directions must be acted upon immediately by the students. In such a context, rote response may prove to be an efficient means of learning, particularly when the goal is development of a specific skill such as pronunciation of a foreign text. Which of us has not polished a Latin text through immediate repetition of troublesome words. Such low-level cognitive skills are probably appropriate in such instances, because the students may yet lack the background and knowledge to make decisions about the correctness of their efforts, or the skills to devise ways of solving the problems without direct teacher intervention.

If, however, the teacher is always solely responsible for decision-making in the choral rehearsal, the students act as mere automatons responding with little independent thought. Such a scenario is incompatible with the current emphasis on teaching critical thinking skills. By its very nature, critical thinking goes far beyond rote learning; hence its development demands a more complex learning environment than that of mere stimulus and response. According to Ennis, cited in *Dimensions of Thinking*, critical thinking is "reasonable, reflective thinking that is focused on deciding what to believe or do. [It] involves both dispositions and abilities" (Marzano et al., 19). Ennis clarifies fourteen dispositions and twelve abilities, the latter ranging from "elementary clarification" to garnering "basic support" to "inferring" and "advanced clarification," among others. This analysis clearly reveals the complexity of critical thinking, thereby reminding us of the need to structure the learning environment accordingly. Teaching for development of critical thinking skills demands that we engage our students in situations where they will be challenged intellectually, not merely expected to comply with our demands.

Before considering how to accomplish the teaching of thinking within the choral rehearsal, we must first distinguish between two contrasting viewpoints about goals for the high school choral class. A teacher's long term goals have a major impact on day-to-day instructional strategies. On the one hand, there is the traditional performance orientation where emphasis is on highly visible skills of the choir; the "curriculum" emerges and is conditioned by the various performing obligations of the group such as the annual holiday concert, ensemble contests, and the spring musical. Teachers involved in this type of program must cover a lot of literature and often the quickest way to teach it is to use the kind of stimulus-response structure mentioned previously. On the other hand, goals that support the development of comprehensive musicianship encompass not only vocal skill development, but also conceptual understanding and aesthetic growth. The curricular framework emerging from such goals as these encompasses a grasp of musical elements along with learning of repertoire as well as development of positive affective responses.

An essential difference between the two kinds of goals is the emphasis on musical independence inherent in the second. The student who learns to function as an independent musician capable of solving musical problems will be better equipped music for personal life-long musical pursuits after high school. Not dependent upon the teacher to control much of his or her musical experience, the graduate of a comprehensive music program may later serve as a valued member of a community or church choir, or to be an otherwise active supporter of the arts. The student who has been denied the development of musical independence at the hands of the performance-only teacher is relegated to a more passive position, musically dependent upon whomever will continue in the role of the high school teacher.

Promoting critical thinking within the choral class, and thus helping students attain goals of musical independence, can be facilitated by development of core thinking skills as outlined in *Dimensions of Thinking* (68). The authors delineate eight categories of core thinking skills: focusing, information-gathering, remembering, organizing, analyzing, generating, integrating, and evaluating. For simplicity's sake, let us divide the hierarchy into three levels: lower, middle, and higher. (See figure 1.) The lowest level incorporates rote learning, where the student relies on memory to recall specific facts like pitch names and key signatures. Because there is a specific body of facts that the learner must acquire, basic memory skills are fundamental. A problem arises, however, when the bulk of one's learning is at this level and the learner does not gain the ability to transfer or apply such facts to new contexts. The middle level of thinking skills goes a step further and requires that the learner organize these facts and concepts, applying what is known to new settings. This is a critical component of problem-solving, where the learner compares the unknown with the known and begins to draw relationships between the two. Problem-solving skills are essential in a world changing as rapidly as ours; new challenges must be faced constantly. Finally, the upper level of core thinking skills, comprising analysis, integration, and evaluation, uses more sophisticated thinking skills that require the learner to assess, draw inferences, synthesize information, and make judgments.

As teachers, we regularly engage in all of these levels, but may not involve our students enough in the process. When we set out to solve a musical problem (for example, to learn and teach a specific piece of music) we rely on our previous knowledge to read the score; we apply what we already know to the new score; we analyze the music and our teaching strategies; we integrate our ideas into new contexts and evaluate the effectiveness of our decisions before, during, and after the rehearsal.

Core Thinking Skills		
Lower Level	*Middle Level*	*Upper Level*
focusing	organizing	analyzing
information	gathering	generating
remembering	integrating	evaluating

Figure 1

It is all too easy to engage the students only at the lowest level of thinking, that is, to emphasize information gathering and remembering skills often in a rote context, where all we expect of the students is to follow directions. Taking the learners beyond that level demands that we structure teaching to accommodate critical thinking and problem-solving strategies such as those we use when preparing for the rehearsal of a new musical work. Doing so takes time. If our goals expand beyond merely having students learn repertoire to include helping students develop thinking skills, we may not initially cover as much repertoire as quickly. In the short term, a problem-solving approach may seem less efficient because it is more time-consuming. On the other hand, if we are truly teaching our students how to learn, they will be able to use more efficient strategies the next time they are faced with a musical problem. Eventually they will be able to learn more quickly. Think, for example, of the teacher who "doesn't have time" to teach students how to read music, yet literally "starts from scratch" and laboriously teaches each voice part separately every time a new piece is introduced. How much more efficient it would be to develop reading skills continuously and see them applied to the learning of new music!

Choral programs that exist to develop comprehensive musical growth and culminate in musical independence are fertile ground for building critical thinking skills. In contrast, programs bounded by excessive performance and public relations demands are less likely to produce critical thinkers unless teaches consciously balance vocal skill development with thinking skill development. Integrating preparation for heavy performance schedules with development of musical independence and critical thinking can be accomplished through careful rehearsal planning.

What kind of rehearsal would accommodate teaching of critical thinking skills and thus development of musical independence? What is needed is a framework on which to structure our planning. One useful model is that proposed by Small (1987, 47) who outlines four ways in which teachers can help students develop critical thinking: (1) structuring "an atmosphere of cognitive challenge"; (2) planning for "cognitive dissonance"; (3) assisting students in developing "a repertoire of questions to activate the reasoning process"; and (4) building toward success in critical thinking. Each of these can function at every stage of the choral rehearsal. A typical rehearsal consists of warmups, work on new material, review, and polishing of familiar music. We will consider these segments in relation to Small's four suggestions.

The warmup period may become an automatic, perfunctory beginning to a rehearsal, relatively meaningless to the students, unless the teacher consciously involves them in the process. Ideally, the warmup is a prime time for developing aural skills, music reading strategies, and concepts of vocal tone, among other objectives. To structure cognitive challenges, the teacher might begin the warmup by having the students view several melodic or rhythmic patterns on the chalkboard and asking them to identify the one(s) played or sung by the teacher. Depending upon the students' level of readiness, these patterns could be written either as graphic representations or traditional notation. Choosing the correct response involves analysis of all possible solutions, and finally, evaluation of the example selected as correct in relation to what was heard. It is essential that the teacher expect the students to be able to give specific reasons for their choices. "Can you find the pattern?" may prompt thinking, but "How do you know that specific pattern matches what you heard?" extends the process further to critical, analytical thinking. Having to verbalize the answer to the second question eliminates mere guessing as the student must synthesize aloud. Lipman (1988, 40) notes that "the improvement of student thinking—from ordinary thinking to good thinking—depends heavily upon students' ability to identify and cite good reasons for their opinions." Once patterns are correctly identified through this process, they may be used as vocalises.

Cognitive challenge can also be injected in the context of typical vocal exercises by teaching students to sing these with little or no piano doubling. Rather than automatically playing the chord for each successive key, challenge the singers to find the next half-step up or down, hum it, and then analyze their efforts as they compare what they hummed with the piano. This kind of listening and evaluation may be time-consuming at first, but certainly will result in improved intonation and musical independence.

Finally, in terms of vocal skills, as the basics of breathing and tone become established, allow the students to function as diagnosticians, listening critically to assess their success. The choir can be divided into sections, each singing for the other group which then makes suggestions for improvement. This kind of assessment can also be done by individual students. It is essential, however, that the students know what the ideal tonal or vocal goal is before engaging in this activity. As Lipman (1988, 40) says, "critical thinking relies upon criteria."

Introducing cognitive dissonance into the warmup may occur in several ways. The teacher might deliberately notate patterns incorrectly, or play one that does not appear on the chalkboard, in order to evaluate students' aural-visual skills. Once the students discern the error, asking them to change the notation to match the sound of the pattern introduces another opportunity for problem-solving. An example related to vocalises would be to exaggerate incorrect vowel formation to reinforce the point that proper shaping of vowels is essential to good choral tone. "What would happen to our tone if you smiled more on that 'ee' vowel?" Performing an example of blatantly incorrect diction would surely put the proper version in perspective!

Facilitating students' analytical questioning skills can occur during the warmup as elsewhere during the rehearsal through modeling. As the teacher questions aloud, the students begin to sense the kinds of reflective processes involved in critical thinking. Reahm (1986, 30) suggests that we "tell the class the thoughts going through (our) mind(s) during the rehearsal." During vocal exercises, for example, we might share a concern with the students: "Sopranos, I hear your tone getting tighter as you sing those high F-sharps. Why do you think that is happening? How could we keep the sound more free?" Eliciting suggestions from the students rather than automatically providing answers ourselves will lead to greater involvement on the singers' parts. With guidance from the teacher, the sopranos could try out alternative solutions, deciding which is most helpful.

Another example of developing questioning skills might occur when making the transition from the warmup to review of familiar repertoire as we pose a question about tonality: "The last exercise we sang ended on a G. How can we get into the key of C major from there?" Concluding that singing up four pitches is one solution would be a point of departure for learning how to change keys without always having to depend on the piano. In developing a repertoire of questions, emphasis on open-ended questions and on the "how" and "why" rather than "what" is helpful in promoting critical thinking skills (Small 1987).

A sense of success results when cognitive challenges are met, when cognitive dissonance is resolved, and when questions lead to satisfying and productive answers. The process rather than the products of critical thinking should earn the teacher's praise; if the students are beginning to probe and reflect in a sincere manner, the fact that they may not always agree with the teacher or come up with the perfect solution is secondary. Music has many "right answers," or very few, depending upon our perspective; weighing the alternatives and choosing the most appropriate requires careful thought.

The remaining portions of the rehearsal, learning of new repertoire and reviewing of familiar material, also offer opportunities for promoting critical thinking within the context of Small's four suggestions. In a well-sequenced rehearsal, warmups should be derived from and lead into the repertoire. Cognitive challenge would be present when the students are asked to find examples of melodies or rhythms from the warmups in the music: "How does the composer of the piece use this example?" "Where does it occur?" "How is it different from (or the same as) the way we performed it earlier in class?"

Similarly, study of the choral text might provide cognitive challenge. The meaning of the poetry can be approached from several angles, including study of the poet as an artist (background, creative output, recurring themes if existent, for example) as well as examination of the particular text of the work being studied (relevant historical context, meaning and interpretation, and relation of words to musical setting). Too often we give the students only our interpretation, implying that there is just one way to perform the music. Furthermore, if we fail even to share with the students how we arrived at that interpretation, we give them no sense of the decision-making process involved in musical performance. Reahm (1986, 30) says that "we owe it to our students to let them know when we make critical and creative decisions about how the music will be performed." Again, thinking aloud is one way of doing this. As students develop their musical knowledge, encouraging them to make decisions about musical dimensions such as tempo, dynamics, and style, based on the text, historical context, or musical structure, can challenge them to function as independent musicians.

Specific instances of cognitive dissonance can be set up either in learning new music or while rehearsing familiar repertoire. Working for expressive interpretation offers many possibilities; proposing deliberately inappropriate solutions to musical problems can challenge the students to question and develop more suitable approaches to performance. For example, rehearsing at a tempo or dynamic level that is inconsistent with the musical style or text may enable students who are temporarily unnerved to come to a more appropriate solution with clear focus and understanding of why a specific tempo is more acceptable. It is essential, of course, to resolve such cognitive dissonance so that confusion about appropriateness of musical responses does not result.

Questioning skills can be developed while learning repertoire as the teacher shares the responsibility of musical decision-making with the students. Again, verbalizing about the process of music learning is essential; "Here is a new piece of music; what do we have to know about it in order to learn it, and how should we start?" Implicit in that question is the structuring of a sequential response to a specific problem. Given the answer, worked out in tandem by students and the teacher, a student can solve similar musical problems independently in the future. Teaching our students the processes involved in musical problem-solving provides them with transferable strategies and skills. To do that, we must use open-ended questions that invite reflection rather than resorting to making statements that elicit automatic and unthinking responses. A rehearsal that moves from one teacher-given command to the next, with no opportunity for student input, is not the setting for developing critical thinking skills. Unfortunately, such a setting seems relatively efficient to many of us, and we lose sight of that valid long-term goal of promoting musical independence.

Students must be persuaded that this approach is beneficial to them. They need to hear the results for themselves. Taping a "before and after" set of performances might permit this. If, for example, we teach a piece by more traditional teacher-directed means with minimal student involvement, and tape that performance in class, we might then begin to challenge the students to think about details of interpreting the music and allow them to try out various ideas. Taping the final agreed-upon version and comparing that with the original could reveal the kind of intensity and commitment that results when the students make the music their own. One hopes that the performance, developed through a cooperative process of reflection and critical thinking, would have greater impact upon the performers than that resulting if they merely follow teacher's directions. This would be one measure of success.

Also essential to the students' feeling of success is recognizing that the teacher is open to suggestions. Allowing students to make musical decisions means giving up some of our power and functioning more as guides than as controllers of the experience. Given our traditional models and training, that may be difficult for many of us at first. Rewarding the process of good critical thinking is essential to its success. That is not to say we must accept every musical suggestion from our students simply because they make the effort. That would be absolving ourselves of the responsibility of teaching and the student from recognizing the total process, including evaluation, that is involved in successful problem solving. We must, however, give our students both the opportunity and the credit for developing their musical independence. If we don't who will?

Developing critical thinking skills in the choral rehearsal is an attainable goal. Given a clear understanding of what constitutes critical thinking, and a framework upon which to build strategies, the choral director at the high-school level can enable students to learn not only musical skills, but thinking skills as well. Doing so may challenge our established patterns of teaching and force us to somewhat alter our planning. Furthermore, it may require that we modify our expectations, at least initially, concerning the amount of repertoire our students will perform in a year. It will certainly require that we reeducate our students, audiences, and administrators! Given the potential rewards, however, not the last of which is greater musical independence for our students, we are obliged to try.

9

MUSICAL THINKING IN THE INSTRUMENTAL REHEARSAL

RICHARD KENNELL

This morning, I observed a student teacher at a nearby high school. She was directing a piece for the first time and the initial results from the students were imprecise and unrefined. The student teacher went to work. As she worked on a crescendo here and a phrasing detail there, the ensemble's precision improved. Individual students improved their scale passages and the accompaniment jelled. I noticed that the ensemble was improving on each reading *in spite of* the directions of the novice teacher! While the student teacher was working at a micro level to improve a few specific trouble spots, the students were independently improving at the macro level of performance. I later commented to the cooperating techer, "You certainly have a very intelligent band...."

What later struck me about this encounter was my selection of the word "intelligent" where I might have been expected to use "well-trained." These students were not "well-trained" in the sense that their director had placed all the notes and nuances for them. No, these students were displaying definite musical independence from their student teacher/conductor. They were solving problems and making musical decisions on their own. Their steady improvement was definitely a demonstration of working musical intelligence rather than mimicking of a student teacher's instructions.

As instrumental music teachers, we are not used to applying an academic term like "intelligence" to our area of expertise. We are much more comfortable with our own musical vocabulary. We prefer to use the word "talent" rather than "intelligence." This division of professional vocabulary represents a very real difference between what we do as ensemble directors and what other teachers do. We sense that our professional lives may be different from our "academic" classroom teaching colleagues.

Our colleagues use textbooks; we prepare individual musical compositions for concerts. They hold discussions; we conduct rehearsals. They give paper and pencil tests; we go to contests. They assign homework; our students practice. Their students study, our students play. Within the semantics of these contrasts lies a sense of the way we view ourselves and are viewed by others. In short, the presentation of music instruction in the schools frequently remains outside the public's expectations for an "academic" discipline.

The title of this chapter is "Musical Thinking in the Instrumental Rehearsal". Thinking is one of "their" terms, not "ours." However, if I borrow a complementary term from our exclusive professional vocabulary and replace thinking with the word *musicianship,* then we'll all relax and feel right at home. The chapter's focus becomes: "How to teach musicianship through instrumental performance." We are all once again on familiar ground!

As music teachers, we have always been involved with the teaching of thinking skills. We have just called it by a different name, musicianship. While our classroom colleagues deal primarily with the world of verbal discourse, we develop a similar set of intellectual skills through the medium of music. Our problem-solving activities involve the decoding of complex musical symbol systems into live musical performances. These problem solving exercises are guided by traditional rules and conventions that have been passed down from generation to generation. Our students learn to apply these rules to new musical situations in order to function independently. The more musical independence our students achieve, the more musical intelligence or musicianship they exhibit.

Over the years, educational researchers have produced a wealth of research with exciting implications for the development of thinking skills in the domain of oral discourse. Some of these strategies and techniques may be useful to music teachers concerned with developing musicianship in their students.

Metacognition and Executive Control

Chapter 2 of this book deals with the importance of helping students gain control of their thinking processes by engaging in metacognition, including maintaining executive control. One aspect of our ensemble performance tradition presents a major problem for the development of executive control processes (planning, evaluation, and regulation) in our students. Quite simply, when we teach, we simultaneously perform. We make music *with* our students. I cannot think of another subject area in which the roles of teacher and student are so intertwined. Our music making is a joint activity between the responsibilities and actions of the teacher and the responsibilities and actions of our students. Traditionally, the teacher selects the music to be performed, plans a set of rehearsals, and monitors the progress toward performance standards. These are examples of executive control processes that we rarely share with our students. We don't share these with our students in two ways. First, we don't reveal our actions and decisions to our students and second, we do not put our students into situations that require them to use these executive control functions in meaningful ways.

Our first task, then, is to consider ways in which the instrumental music teacher might transfer executive control process experience from teacher to student. Initially, we can briefly discuss the criteria for selecting music with our students. We can reveal our choices by explaining why we picked one piece over another.

As students become aware of the process involved in choice, we can assign small groups of students to participate in the music selection process for the ensembles in which they perform. We can make these students especially responsible for identifying specific goals for the next rehearsal as well as for determining the performance standard to be achieved. It is in the interaction between teacher and students in such planning activities that the teacher's executive control processes become accessible to the student.

Another possibility is to assign students to chamber music groups. These chamber music ensembles could gradually become totally responsible for the selection of literature, the preparation of rehearsals, and the public presentation of their work. This independent activity forces to student to exercise executive control processes in a meaningful way.

Problem Solving

Music performance requires that basic skills be automatic. Teaching music also involves the automaticity of numerous decision-making and problem-solving functions. As we exercise these automated skills in front of our students, the fundamentals are usually invisible.

An example of this is sight reading. When the teacher opens a score for the first time, he or she employs a personal routine to retrieve significant information from the printed page. Try making a list of all the questions you ask yourself upon first exposure to a score. Your list will no doubt include many of these questions:

1. Have I ever seen or heard this piece before? Am I familiar with the melody?
2. What is the key signature? Are there any changes of key? Is the work melodic or textural? Where is the melody and accompaniment?
3. What is the time signature? Does the time signature remain the same or does it change? What is the tempo marking? Are there any changes in tempo?
4. Are there clearly defined sections? What is the character of each section?
5. What are the stylistic features? What changes in texture occur? Is the work for full ensemble, a chamber group, or a soloist?

By the time we actually begin to read this new piece with our instrumental ensemble, we have already answered these questions. Our answers helped form a specific schema or mental blueprint of this work that we will use in rehearsal. When we ask our student ensembles to sight-read, however, how many of us take the time to share these specific musical problem-solving strategies with our students? These are invisible to our students as we begin work on a new composition.

In rehearsals, therefore, we need to reveal our personal strategies for solving musical problems. In approaching *any* musical problem—sight reading, ensemble balance, precision, rhythm problems and the like—we need to unlock the "automatic" code, which we use immediately but which is invisible to our students.

Have you ever noticed how truly outstanding studio teachers of music performance will offer their students several possible strategies for solving musical problems? How many times have we heard studio teachers say, "This works best for me but you may also want to try..."? I am suggesting that as teachers of ensemble performance, we also need to be collectors of musical problem-solving strategies that we can disseminate to our students. As we disseminate these problem-solving skills to our students we make them more "intelligent" as musicians and thus foster musical independence. It is this musical independence that is, after all, a significant life-long benefit of music participation (Olson 1978).

Creativity

Musical performance is a "re-creative" experience. Performers transform the limited instructions provided by the composer's notation into a live expression of the composer's creation. This transformation involves an interpretation of written symbols to which we also bring a wealth of common-practice knowledge and understanding. But many of the creative decisions involved in this re-creation process are either assigned to the exclusive role of the teacher or are internal and are therefore invisible to the student, as are problem-solving decisions.

Furthermore, our rich ensemble tradition has produced a rather restricted view of music making. The music experience for most instrumental music students consists only of performance. They seldom solve musical problems as composers or make musical decisions as listeners. Yet, we know that for most of our students, listening will be the predominant mode of musical involvement and enjoyment for the rest of their lives. Our school music-making experiences, therefore, must somehow include creating, listening, and evaluating, as well as performing.

There are a number of creative possibilities for instrumental music students short of the "write your own overture" assignment. One of my personal favorites is found in the series *A Contemporary Primer for Band* by Sydney Hodkinson (1973). This series introduces basics of interpreting graphic music composition. The primer can be introduced as early as junior high school, and it encourages students to write their own graphically represented compositions. Student compositions can be easily duplicated and performed. This provides an excellent opportunity for the student composer to teach the new work to the student ensemble.

Another pseudo-creative exercise I have found to be very successful is the "reconstruct the melody" activity. I was first introduced to this activity by an high school English teacher who was using a "reconstruct the poem" exercise. The principle is the same in either medium. An unfamiliar poem or melody is cut up into brief phrases. These phrases are randomized and labeled. The student's task is then to examine each phrase and to attempt to reconstruct the original order. By considering sequences, line direction, cadence points, and other internal musical details, students are quite capable of reconstructing unfamiliar melodies.

It is ironic that there are so few opportunities to listen to music within our traditional instrumental music ensembles. We are so busy making music that there is little time to listen to it. Listening to music, however, provides an ideal human experience for exercising core thinking skills—focusing, information gathering, remembering, organizing, analyzing, generating, integrating and evaluating—that are the basic components of other higher-level mental processes. (Marzano et al. 1988, 69).

Music listening allows us to use all of these core skills. For example, as the rehearsal proceeds students can be asked to determine, through listening, "Which instruments have the melody? Where have you heard this line before? Can you think of another accompaniment figure that would compliment this melodic line? How far apart are the highest and lowest pitches in this melody? From where in the melody line does the accompaniment figure come? Which note in this cadence sounds like it doesn't belong?"

The Teacher's Role

The music teacher should always be a model for successful music thinking skills. As we display personal commitment, positive attitudes, and intense attention we are communicating successful thinking strategies to our students. As individual students exercise these qualities and achieve success, we need to point these out to our students. We need to bring these control processes to the attention of our students whenever possible.

The music teacher should also model diverse musical roles. Our students should have opportunities to see us engage in different music experiences: conducting, performing, listening, and composing or arranging. As we make creative links between music and other subjects, we provide a model for our students' future lives.

The kind of instrumental music program that draws on musicianship-fostering strategies will be very different from the traditional instrumental music program most often seen today. It will include a greater variety of learning contexts, place the teacher in new and demanding roles, and offer students a broader range of musical experiences. In short, instrumental music education will take on a totally new definition.

The historical traditions of the school music program emulating the college and military band have served us well over the past sixty years. There are indications, however, that music teachers across this nation are seeking new answers to our professional dilemmas: What shall we teach? Whom shall we teach? How shall we teach?

To illustrate some of the kinds of changes in the focus and structure of instrumental music programs, let me briefly describe one of the high schools that I visit to supervise student teachers. It is a "typical" instrumental music program in a "typical" town. What is atypical, however, is the consistently high level of musicianship displayed by its students. At this school, the teaching staff has established a set of after-school musicianship requirements. These requirements include some music theory, creative, and performance-skill enhancing activities. Each student's class grade is tied to this out-of-class work.

Whether the superior performing skills of this band can be attributed to this musicianship-fostering program is subject to debate. I point to this program only as it is representative of a growing number of instrumental music programs around the country that are redefining the expectations of instrumental music education. It provides its students with experiences that not only improve their performance skills, but that also improve their musicianship skills, their ability to process musical information, and thus their ability to become independent musicians.

I also point to this program because it demonstrates that high performance standards need not be compromised by attention to musicianship fostering activities. Indeed, personal musicianship skill development complements our traditional goals of excellence in music performance.

10

MUSICAL THINKING IN THE SPECIAL EDUCATION CLASSROOM

BETTY WELSBACHER

Walk into the office of the director of special education in an east coast city, where hundreds of teachers of exceptional children are hired, scheduled, monitored, and trained. Try the educational building in a midwestern county seat, where the dozen or so scattered classrooms of a rural cooperative educational district are administered. Find the room housing the desk of the small city's assistant superintendent, whose several duties include the overseeing of special classes. At each of these places, one individual or many will be juggling the elements that determine the education of the special children under their supervision, threading together the vastly varied pieces: curricula, transportation, state and federal guidelines, legal contingencies, workups, testing and placement, hot lunches, certification standards, paraprofessional supply, staffings, validation, individual education program (I.E.P.) budgets. Acronyms fly like feathers: EMH, DDK, HI, VI, PI and SLD; last year's PSA is this year's BD, and neither is easy. TMH and SMH must be relocated, and neither is cheap. With nationwide special teaching, so varied in location and situation, with even more variables than occur in "regular" education, with so many children who themselves are wildly different from each other, is there even a chance that teachers can be concerned about such an unlikely topic, for these students, as helping them learn to think?

Of course teachers can be, and must be. Often the hardest part is simply realizing that it is possible. The learning theory of choice for special education children has been, for so long, basic behaviorism that the idea of "thinking" rather than "imitating and remembering" may be difficult for special education teachers to envision. But music teachers have a singular advantage over their colleagues; they are literally coming from a different place. The subject that we bring to our exceptional students is an art form—not arithmetic or writing or vocational training—but music. As with all of our students, but especially for special education children, the ultimate "prize" of their education can only be to develop skills that will help them learn to learn. And, even more than with other children, music for them may be a better arena than traditional subject areas are, for "learning to learn" skills to take root.

The Reality of Music

In earlier parts of this volume we noted the "reality" of the music experience. A special student is involved in music in exactly the same way (though of course at a different level) as anyone else. Music *is* music, not a model or an approximation of it. "The medium is the message," and it requires the same processes and practices for all who engage in it. Further, music is authentically and totally accessible to special individuals, even if they lack language, as is no other subject area. Children are free to develop thinking skills to "learn to learn" music, even if they are denied this possibility in other subject areas. Music provides the "reality" of being exactly the same to them as to anyone, and the opportunity for learning its content and appropriate behaviors without being penalized for poor language skills.

But is this prize actually possible for special students? After all, aren't they "special" because of a loss—of vision, movement, hearing; of perceptual clarity, of understanding? And don't they all, to some extent, have a lesser ability to "think"?

Unlocking Thinking Skills

As these words are written, ticket are sold out for the homecoming concert on this campus, an event that will present Ray Charles, a recent Lincoln Center Honoree. Greg Louganis has just won two "golds" for diving—an Olympic first. Christopher Nolan's novel, *In the Eye of the Clock* has won the prestigious Whitbread literary award in England. Stephen Hawkins' *A Brief History of Time* is a bestseller here as everywhere, and Phyllis Froelich has won yet another acting award for her latest performance. These are real winners; their prizes are tangible: brass or gold or parchment. Their disabilities, except for one, are among those acronyms of the administrative offices: Charles's blindness, Louganis's learning disability; the writers' physical disabilities; Nolan's cerebral palsy—so severe that at age twenty-one he can communicate only with his eyes; Hawkins's ALS ("Lou Gehrig's disease"), which has finally immobilized and silenced him; Froelich's deafness. All but Hawkins spent some or all of their educational years in special education classrooms. Of them, only Charles is a professional musician, but few would argue that all are artists. There is little doubt that their tangible prizes, and the skills and talents that have produced them, are ultimate outcomes of that more intrinsic prize, knowing how to think. It would seem, then, that thinking can indeed be learned by special students, at least in some cases!

Of course, these extraordinary people can be considered as remarkable "exceptions to the rules." But if they are exceptions, what has made them exceptional?

Recall once more the thinking skills that are the topic of this volume: critical and creative thinking, the familiar core skills—focusing, organizing, remembering, and the rest. Across the board, in nearly all exceptionality groupings, the majority of the special students assigned to these categories really are capable, to a greater or lesser extent, of utilizing almost all of these stated skills under most circumstances. But we are prone to notice odd gaps, unexpected holes, a displacement of order, perhaps such as erratic performance behaviors, unnerving disparities, and scattering. Individual skills exist in abundance, sometimes prodigiously: the trainable-mentally-retarded (TMH) girl who can sing every line of every verse of every song she's ever learned; the central-language-disordered boy who drowns us with endless facts about his pet subject; the deaf child whose dances are as eloquent as words; the illiterate, dyslexic eighth grader who has taught himself to play the organ by ear. Yet the skills are often locked in: the TMH girl can't speak any of the lines of music she sings; the language-disordered boy absorbs nothing about other topics; the deaf child does not grasp language, even signed.

What is missing? Where is the breakdown? What have our prize-winners mastered that eludes our students, keeping them from using in meaningful ways the thinking skills that they have acquired?

Among our "winners," self-awareness and self-monitoring are as fine-tuned as is a musical instrument. They have become expert in metacognition. At the sold-out Ray Charles concert, no song was ever performed exactly as it had been before, for this new audience on this new instrument. In the Olympic pool, Louganis's perfect dives meant perfect conscious control and knowledge of body movement and of surrounding space, one split second after another. Nolan's amazing word-images and Hawkins's pure thought caught in words almost define metacognition: awareness of cognitive process *becomes* their product.

But for most of the students in our classes, this is the last, the hardest thing to grasp. Perhaps for some it is impossible. The inability to monitor one's own thinking very nearly describes the basic disability of many exceptional children. In *South Pacific,* Nellie Forbush tells us that, "you have to be carefully taught." Her song is of pride and prejudice, but her thesis is correct for our topic, too. Special children usually cannot monitor their own learning; they cannot learn by osmosis. But they can learn, and they do respond to being carefully taught. With music, they often can learn the skills of metacognition, providing a key to unlock their potential thinking skills.

Metacognition: The Key

In earlier sections of this volume we became familiar with key words associated with metacognition: self control, tracking, self monitoring, judgment, consciousness, knowledge, awareness, interaction, attending, and commitment.

At the beginning of this chapter we touched on exceptionalities, the set of characteristics that differentiates one group of exceptional persons from another. We shall limit our discussion of their relationship to metacognition to the exceptionalities that are usually present in most schools. We will not discuss early childhood handicapped children; gifted, talented and creative (GTC) classes; or classes for autistic children. Most ECH classes are made up of young children who clearly need to receive the same kinds of musical experiences as their early childhood and kindergarten counterparts in regular classes, with the same kind of adaptations as would be used with older children of their apparent exceptionalities. Although gifted children are considered exceptional in many states, taking part in IEP and placement committee decisions and receiving special curricular programs, they are obviously not deficient in thinking skills as a group (thought a number of gifted children may also have disabilities of types not involving intelligence per se). Autistic children are of several "syndrome groups," not all demonstrating the same degree of central language deficit and emotional withdrawal; their problems are of such an individual nature that it seems unwise to categorize them here as a group.

The exceptionalities to be considered in this chapter are:

Developmentally disabled groups:

Educable mentally handicapped (EMH)

Trainable mentally handicapped (TMH)

Severely multiply handicapped (SMH)

This last acronym can be misleading; some systems use this designation to identify multiply physically handicapped children who have no intelligence loss at all. Most systems, however, consider these children to be severely developmentally disabled, and to also have other disabilities.

Traditional sensory loss groups:

Visually impaired or blind (VI)

Hearing impaired (HI)

Other: such as those with cerebral palsy, spina bifida and multiple sclerosis.

Neurologically/perceptually damaged:

Neurologically dysfunctioning, brain damaged (ND)

Learning disabled (LD). (LD is an umbrella term, usually applied to those with visual, auditory, or motor perceptual deficiencies or language problems, but who have potentially normal intelligence.)

Emotionally/behaviorially disturbed:

Emotionally disturbed (ED)

Behavior disordered (BD)

Personal and social adjustment problems (PSA)

Metacognitive Skills as Fundamental

For some exceptional children, difficulties with metacognitive skills lie at the core of their disability. Two such groups are the emotionally/behaviorially disturbed, and the neurologically dysfunctioning/learning disabled.

The list of key words delineating metacognitive skills could define the problems of emotionally and behaviorally disturbed students. If an ED child could monitor his central thinking skills he or she would not be disturbed. To a teacher or a caregiver, work with these students is delicate, full of missteps, and fragile as a cobweb. But for the students themselves, gaining those stated skills is the only game in town. They cannot function normally without them. For teachers, approaching the skills as thinking strategies is a different, and potentially more productive, way of engaging these children in their own learning than is the usual method. The traditional management model for emotionally disturbed children is behavioral modification, which to be effective must permeate every aspect of the school day and perhaps beyond.

Metacognition traffics in questions: "How? What? When? If, then?" As the student explores and practices the questions, there may be answers—the student's own. Perhaps such questions are self-generated; there might be self monitoring; a modicum of self control may enter the process. These are the same goals the traditional method is seeking.

There are more likely to be statements than questions in behavioral modification or similar management approaches: "Control yourself," "Remember the consequences if you...." In such situations the payoff for the student tends to be negative: "Control yourself—and your privileges won't be removed"; "Remember the consequences, and you won't have to go to 'time-out'." Approached as the acquisition of thinking skills, however, the fiddler calls a different tune. Music, by nature, is nonthreatening, the statements are replaced by questions to be explored, and self-monitoring in this atmosphere does not carry the implied anxiety load of expected failure. The payoff is positive. The elusive feeling of doing something well—the "prize" of education—may occur if thinking skills can be attained.

ND and LD students, as outcomes of their disabilities, often cannot interpret sensory input accurately. They literally receive faulty information; thus have difficulty in focusing and attending. For quite different reasons than those of ED students, these children also find the lack of metacognitive understanding at the core of their disabilities. If perceptually handicapped children could monitor the input of their sensory pathways and receive it without distortion, they would not be disabled either. Here the problem is not so volatile or erratic as with ED students, but is the result of mixed signals, improperly transmitted neural patterns, and incomplete or distorted sensory reception. Now metacognition becomes a matter of self-recognition of problem areas; trial-and-error attempts to "trick" or circumvent faulty perceptual tracks, undertaken knowingly and deliberately by the student.

The fifth-grade LD child who has trouble with midline crossing because of motoric perception and laterality problems falls apart when presented with a crossed-arms finger-snapping pattern in a hand-jive activity. At first he denies it happened and refuses to try again. But, asked to become aware of how it really feels to do the exercise, and to try to figure out a way to fool his arms and hands into doing it, he tries again—first without crossing at all, then a little at a time, crossing and moving tentatively as he monitors his own movement. In time he may be successful to some degree; he'll not be perfect, and the movement won't always be comfortable. But he'll have done it! And next time he'll remember his self-learning and find the activity less difficult. The whole affair has been much easier because of the security provided by the music itself, and the carefully monitored practice of the skill. For LD children, such self-awareness, attention, and self control are the only known ways for them to alleviate the effects of their disability.

Metacognitive Skill Learning

For children with other exceptionalities, serious problems with metacognition may exist, but they are not so much at the very heart of their problem as with the previously named groups. Developmentally disabled and visually, hearing, and physically disabled children tend to live in an educational world that seldom reaches beyond imitation and a rote accumulation of certain facts. These special education children seldom are given the opportunity to exercise judgment or to make personal choices. This is understandable, given the necessity for learning academic material correctly. Arithmetic, grammar, and spelling are not subjects with which one can take liberties. But music is ripe with circumstances allowing these children to engage in thinking opportunities unavailable to them elsewhere. When such children are first offered chances to exercise judgment in music situations, they may not comprehend them. "Which way sounds better to you?" Sounds *better*? There is a "better"? And I can choose it?

This is a new idea. It deals not with creative or critical thinking skills at this point, though those are clearly where it can lead; it deals initially with developing skills of metacognition: "What if *I*...?" "Maybe *I'd* better..."; these questions predicate the existence of control, of choice. Choices require options. Options mean choosing and knowing why, judging and recognizing the reasons. Dealing with choices and judgments in music is a beginning for all children of metacognitive thought, both simple and sophisticated. It will be effective at all levels of a child's abilities and skills. It can take place in a music setting easily and naturally; and this may well be the only setting in the education program where such options are available.

Strategies for Metacognition

How can we teach the skills of metacognition to our special students? In chapter 2 of this book, Pogonowski speaks of students who see themselves as "designers of their own learning." In so many ways, society and the schools that mirror it seem to believe that if that descriptor is true at all, it certainly does not apply to these children who, in common parlance, "don't learn." We know they do learn; and we can teach them the skills of metacognition by relinquishing a bit of our "ownership" of the music and the musical experience. We can stop spooning it out, a carefully measured dose at a time and give music back to these children, providing the materials they need, carefully constructing schema to move down roads of discovery, and stepping back when they arrive to let the learning be theirs.

We can place them in new roles:

As translators of sounds into meaningful patterns: Show with your fingers how rain sounds...more rain...less...make a rainshower...a hard storm. What made it sound like rain? How did you change it? What if you had used something else for the rain?

As discoverers and makers of instruments and sounds: Search for and find, just in this room, things that can be instruments. Find many ways to make different sounds with them. When in this song would be a good place to play them? When would be a poor place? Why? Which of your new instruments would be better? Why?

As makers and arrangers of music: "There's new snow today, on the playground! Let's say snow words...sing snow words...put snow words together to show how the snow felt. Let's use your new instruments to play snow words; will they all sound right? Which are the best? Why? Can you find some new ones that sound right? Let's make a music piece from our words and sounds. How? What shall we do? Where shall we do it? When? What shall be first?"

As performers: "Let's tape the two ways you decided to arrange your song; once with instruments and once with soft clapping. Are they just the way you want them? Fast enough or too fast? How about loudness? All the way through or not? Who can think of a way to clap and still hear the words of our song?"

As critics: "Which of the two performances that you taped do you think sounds best? Why? Would it be better if you tried another way? What way? Here are two different ways that an orchestra played a piece of music. Which do you prefer? Why, why, why?"

There is nothing new here: These are basic self-generating approaches that are used often in regular classes. We use them less often with special children, perhaps because their lack of traditional academic skills may have persuaded us that music is unavailable to them, too. But it takes only a little experimenting to discover the satisfaction, for both student and teacher, of an approach that uses metacognitive skill development.

For not-very-big adjustments in the usual strategies for working with special children, the outcomes can be disproportionately large. With regular children, developing thinking skills at all levels can improve their school progress, and can carry over into their futures. With special education children, possession of these skills is often the difference between succeeding in anything and failing. In terms of individual children's lives, the stakes are high and rewards can be sizeable. In this world, no one wins them all; but control over even some of the tools of thinking can make it possible for these children, as well as their regular classmates, to be the designers of their own learning.

11

MUSICAL THINKING IN THE TEACHER EDUCATION CLASSROOM

MARY PAUTZ

Music education has always been blessed with caring, competent, and conscientious people in the teacher-education field. The success and creativity of music programs throughout the country is a testament to their efforts to instruct and inspire. In order to continue to improve the field of music education, however, those who prepare teachers must remain knowledgeable regarding developments in educational reform. Knowledge of how people learn, and how to use that understanding when planning classroom instruction, is of the utmost importance. While much of the latest emphasis on thinking is a refinement of earlier writings, the focus on teaching the dimensions of thinking at a conscious level is, for most of us, a new experience.

Teaching thinking skills and processes is valuable to instructor and student alike. The "teacher of teachers" profits in the clarification of the how and why of teaching. Many actions that have become second nature and are performed automatically (such as writing a lesson plan or teaching a song) must now be analyzed in order to help the student in the methods class grasp the underlying thought processes. The future teacher profits in his or her own personal development and in awareness of the thinking process, particularly metacognition. The greatest gift that we can give future teachers is to instill in them a habit of thoughtfulness, of monitoring their own thinking.

A thoughtful music educator will not "jump on every bandwagon" that comes along but will evaluate and analyze critically the merits of each proposal. A thoughtful music educator will search for meaningful ways to incorporate the many new ideas learned at conventions into an organized curriculum rather than viewing these ideas as simply ready-made lesson plans for the next week, with no thought of sequence or follow through. A thoughtful music educator will be convinced that he or she can solve problems rather than wait to be told what to do. A thoughtful music educator will choose music on the merits of its aesthetic quality, its value to develop concepts, and its age appropriateness rather than on its "cuteness" or audience appeal. Finally, a thoughtful music educators will know why a particular lesson, rehearsal scheme, or instructional strategy worked well, will know how to make necessary adjustments in teaching as it is unfolding and will search for knowledge and skills rather than gimmicks and tricks. In other words, the thoughtful music educator will be a lifelong expert learner and thus a master teacher.

It is time, then, that we declare as members of the music education profession that we:

- value creative thinking as much as performance.
- value critical thinking as much as skill acquisition.
- will help prospective teachers develop a repertoire of metacognitive and cognitive strategies as well as a repertoire of music.
- will provide, and insist upon, as much practice time in core thinking skills as in conducting skills.
- will make problem solving and decision making as salient a factor in discussions on lesson planning as the musical activity to be enjoyed.

These resolutions can and must be achieved without adding more course work to the curriculum. They can be incorporated into existing courses so that future music teachers are prepared to lead classes and rehearsals that are alive with both the *sound of music* and *the sound of thinking*. One is not exclusive of the other: Making of music (whether by creating, describing, or performing) need not be devoid of thinking on the part of students. Goodlad (1983, 8–9) found that more often than not it is the arts educator rather than the student who makes the decisions in the learning process and that music instruction, like other areas of education, focuses on "lower cognitive processes." Band, chorus and orchestra rehearsals must encompass more than performance and skill acquisition; general music class in middle and secondary schools must be more than mini-versions of college music appreciation lectures and elementary general music must be more than "singing time." Time must be devoted to the understanding of musical concepts and their contribution to the expressiveness of music in order to achieve true comprehensive musicianship. This education can happen only when conscious planning and sequencing are of the first priority. De Lorenzo (1987, 20–21) concluded that "the higher levels of musical understanding come not only from active interaction with musical materials but also from well-designed questions that help students make sense of their experiences."

Acquisition of such higher levels of understanding cannot be left to chance. Lip service regarding lofty ideals will produce no change. It is the conscious teaching of this framework of thinking defined by the authors of *Dimensions of Thinking* that is the responsibility of each person charged with teacher education. The remainder of this chapter will be devoted to suggestions that can be incorporated into existing music education courses.

Field Experience

Rather than merely fulfilling university or state certification requirements for field experience in a perfunctory manner: assigning music majors to be physically present in classrooms for a certain number of hours, field experience should be a great opportunity for students to acquire and practice core thinking skills and processes.

One of the problems facing the supervisor of field experiences is the difficulty in knowing what the student is observing. Without direction, most students will report only the obvious: "The band did a warmup and then began at measure 45 of the march." "The second graders learned a dance and the song 'Free to Be Me'." "The Teacher stopped the chorus and rehearsed the tenors separately." "A group of students were fooling around in the back of the room during the filmstrip."

Students need to learn how to observe in order to make the field experience worthwhile. Students must be encouraged to evaluate, to look beneath the surface to see what works in the classroom, what doesn't work and, most importantly, why something either works or doesn't. Prior to assigning students to individual classes, a videotape of a music class or rehearsal should be viewed by all. A log of the observations made of the class should be recorded by the college supervisor as well as by each student. After the logs are compared and discussed, the videotape should be viewed again. This activity could be repeated (with different lessons) several times during the semester. Attention would be focussed on the improvement of quality observations. The advantage of a videotaped lesson over an observation in a "live" classroom is that the tape can be stopped to predict, to evaluate, to analyze, to refocus. Questions such as "What do you think would have improved the situation?", "How did the teacher model metacognition?", and "Would you have stopped the group? Why or why not?" will allow students to become thinking participants rather than passive observers. By using a videotape for all to observe, the teacher can also help students practice making observations.

During observation times, students should be encouraged to practice metacognitive strategies by asking themselves, "Am I aware of the emotional climate that is influencing this situation?" or by reminding themselves, "I can't get so involved in the music making that I forget to watch how the teacher achieves that magical moment." They need to ask themselves, "Why am I usually upset when I observe band during first hour? Is it because the kids are so disrespectful, because the instruments aren't tuned, because of all the interruptions over the PA system or because the rehearsal is so disjointed?" Students need to remind themselves to watch for cues that will indicate whether or not the teacher is modeling thinking strategies.

Instead of a minute-by-minute detailing of the class activities, the observation log should allow the student to practice core thinking skills of analyzing, generating, integrating and evaluating. To facilitate this type of observation, the students should be directed to include some of the following observations, perhaps concentrating on different questions at different times." "The primary objective was...."

"It was achieved by...."

"Understanding of the concept of...was developed by...."

"In addition to the concept, the skills being developed were...."

"I was impressed with... because it...."

"If I were the teacher today, I would change...because...."

"I think the reason the teacher ignored the late student was...."

"If I were a student in this class, I would...."

"If I were a supervisor or principal I would praise...."

"The teacher guided the thinking process by...."

"Thinking strategies shared by the teacher included...."

"Examples of praise given by the teacher included praise for thinking such as...."

"The teacher modelled musicianship by..., and modelled thinking by...."

"The performance was musical (or nonmusical) because...."
"The warmup was related to...."
"The class was brought to closure by...."
"If I were the substitute for the next day with this group, I would...."
"If this class continues to make this type of progress they...."

Assigning students to observe as teams or pairs to do identical observations and then asking them to exchange observation logs and comment on each other's notes can encourage thinking. Another possibility is to assign students in pairs for observation, but each with a different task. One student is to focus on the learning experience from the students' point of view; the other is to observe with attention focused on the teacher's point of view. Together they compile a single log.

To ensure further value in these field experiences, students must be provided with opportunities to observe both sequential development by visiting the same class or performance group each time they meet for a period of several weeks. They should also observe as many different teachers as possible in order to become aware of multiple teaching styles.

Seminars that accompany field experience should include discussion of the role of the teacher as manager, executive, mediator in cognitive processing, and as expert learner. (For further information on this topic see Chapter 7 of *Dimensions of Thinking*.) Traditional topics such as discipline, motivation, curriculum, and grading, can be subsumed under discussion of each of these roles. If at all feasible, arrangements should be made so that teachers who are observed have an opportunity to meet with the seminar group to answer questions, share strategies, discuss rehearsal goals, review lesson plans, and so on.

Methods Courses

Everyone who teachers a methods course is convinced that there is already insufficient time to teach what needs to be taught. (One sometimes wonders if future dentists are sent out with a single course in "drilling"!) Rather than considering the idea of adding more content entitled, "dimensions of thinking musically" to the already crowded syllabus, perhaps we need to look at the content to be taught and incorporate the ideas of thinking through presentation of that material. It may mean eliminating some of the favorite personal anecdotes of "this worked for me" and singing a few less songs; it will definitely mean restructuring the class from a traditional lecture format to more discussion and problem solving in order to provide more time for students to think, to discuss, and to experiment.

What are some of the traditional content areas within a general music methods class and how could these dimensions be incorporated? The following suggestions are not meant to be all inclusive; rather they are a starting point for consideration.

Lesson planning. Many music teachers consider lesson planning completed when the page numbers of the songs have been chosen. As instructors of methods classes we need to ask ourselves, "How do we prepare students to write plans?" Perhaps we are unwittingly contributing to the problem by expecting that the process is somehow learned by osmosis. Lesson plans need to be developed in class. Students must have multiple opportunities over the entire semester to observe and determine the components of lesson planning. They will benefit from examples provided by the instructor as he or she talks through the thought process. Other sample activities might include observing a videotaped lesson. Students are then asked to construct the lesson plan and then compare it to the plan that was written by the instructor teaching the lesson. Another assignment might be to provide a lesson plan with the first and last steps given. The assignment, "prepare two different plans using the same first and last step." Another discussion might revolve around the comparison of lesson plans using the same music (such as "America") from three different music textbook series, or to compare three plans that all focus on development of the same concept while using different music. Class time in which lesson plans are analyzed to determine the cognitive thinking strategies to be employed by children at each step is time well spent!

Sequencing musical concepts. Students are given a hypothetical situation such as, "You are hired for a position. At the end of the final interview the curriculum specialist says, 'By the way, the music curriculum must be rewritten by January first.' Short of resigning on the spot, how will you proceed?" Within the methods class, students need to have experience with sequencing and curriculum building. They will need to define the problem, set the goals, and gather information. "How often do the classes meet? What are the priorities? What other expectations (such as programs, musicals, or contests) are there? What resources are available?" Students will need to consult state curriculum guides, "Concept Banks," and other curricular materials. In so doing they will begin to use the core thinking skills of classification and ordering, among others. After much analysis, they will need to begin to integrate by summarizing and restructuring. When the final draft is composed, their evaluation skills will help them accept or reject their initial ideas. Another possibility would be to assign each student to draw up a long-range timeline for teaching a single element, such as harmony or timbre.

Methodologies. Instead of teaching facts and techniques of the various methodologies, the time could be spent delving into the underlying assumptions of individual methodologies. What a place to use critical thinking! Each methodology (such as Kodály, Orff, Dalcroze, Generative, Gordon, or Suzuki) could be assigned to a group of students to research. A discussion of the goals and principles of each will be drawn up as well as commonalities and differences among methodologies. A debate might be held on the "superiority" of each methodology. Students would have not only a knowledge of the methodologies but also an understanding of how one evaluates new approaches.

Materials. Play roles as members of a committee of music teachers from a school district who must make a decision on which music textbook series to purchase. Criteria are established by the group, the study is made, discussion is held, and the vote taken. Again, there are multiple benefits. In the analysis stage, students will become familiar with the song and listening repertoire. As they read through lesson plans, they are acquiring teaching strategies as well as critiquing the development of the plans as they occur in the teacher's guide. They are forced to think about curricular sequence. In the discussion, they must be able to defend their choices.

Musical skill acquisition. Instead of simply learning a repertoire of specific folk dances or dance steps, learning to play the autoharp and recorder, or learning how to perform Orff ensembles, time will also be spent learning things such as how the folk dances can be incorporated into a lesson plan on form; how autoharp performance skills can be taught as part of a lesson series focusing on the relationship of melody to harmony; and how to help children create their own ensembles.

Knowledge of the learner. After reading about physical, emotional, and intellectual differences among age groups of children, incorporate the application of this knowledge into observations of a general music class or band rehearsal. Students will be requested to make observations about individuals and document their observations by reference to points made in their assigned reading.

Creation of materials. Students should be assigned to prepare a learning center for independent or small-group work. Instead of simply handing it into the teacher to grade, arrangements should be made for the centers to be set up and critiqued by other classmates, using criteria established by the class in advance. Another possibility would be to incorporate this assignment into the field experience and, when possible, set the center up in a general music classroom for the pupils to use. Evaluation of success would be related to the success of the pupils in accomplishing the task for which the center had been designed.

Practice of teaching skills. Ideally, a practicum should be arranged in tandem with the methods class, with the same person serving as instructor of both. Providing students with scripted lesson plans prior to the observation will enable them to think through the lesson planning process. As the semester proceeds, more and more responsibility for learning must be turned over to the students. Rather than receiving the lesson plan in advance, they write up the observation log as a lesson plan. Later they may be asked to write the follow-up lesson. Eventually they must become involved in actually planning a lesson and teaching it. A key portion of the practicum should be for them to keep a log in which they try to describe the thinking process they undertook as they prepared the lesson, as well as when they were teaching. In other words, they should be guided to keep a metacognitive log.

Student Teaching

Cooperating teachers must be selected not only by the intonation of the choral group, the blend of the instruments, the lack of discipline problems, the number of first in contests or the conducting art of the teacher, but also on the ability of that teacher to involve students in a balanced curriculum of performing, describing, and creating that forces them to make decisions, solve problems, evaluate, and synthesize.

Lesson plans and rehearsal plans must be required of student teachers in sufficient detail so that the objective, the materials, the entry behaviors, the cognitive strategies to be employed and the flow of the class period is evident from the written material. Questions should be prepared in advance and written out. The student teacher must plan for transfer within the lesson. He or she must be asked to evaluate the learning of the students, the teaching act, and the preparation and execution of the lesson plan. Audio- and videotapes of the students teaching can be used as vital evaluative tools. The student teacher must chart progress towards long-range goals.

Every person involved in teacher education needs to pose the questions raised by the authors of *Dimensions of Thinking:* "Am I clear about what I am trying to accomplish? Am I well informed about the topic? What sources have I consulted? have I considered a variety of points of view or only those I favor? am I doing this as well as I possibly can?" (Marzano et al. 1988, 29)

There will be missteps in teaching cognitive and metacognitive strategies. Sternberg (1987, 456–59) warns of the danger of a teacher who tries to teach students to think by telling them "what the problem is, how to pose the problem, the way (rarely ways) to solve the problem and then leaves it to the students to do the 'problem solving'." He points out that the teacher has done the most important thinking and has only left the routine aspects of problem solving to be completed by the student. Sternberg further states that if it is true that there is no better way to learn than to teach, "then we must let students teach themselves to a great extent. We need to serve as facilitators, and we must recognize that we, too, are learners" (459).

12

MUSICAL THINKING AND TECHNOLOGY

BRIAN MOORE

Although the idea of thinking within the context of school learning is certainly not new, it has undergone a recent revival of interest. Critical and creative thinking, metacognition, and thinking processes such as problem solving and decision making are receiving attention on the part of teachers and curriculum designers. This renewed interest, as evidenced by this book and *Dimensions of Thinking,* reflects the tremendous technological changes that continue to influence our society and, thus, education. An understanding of these changes provides an important context for the effective development of musical thinking via technology.

A Society in Transition

The influence of technology has resulted in our shifting from an industrial society, with its emphasis upon the physical and mechanical work, to an information society,

111

which stresses mental and electronic work. John Naisbitt in his book *Megatrends* echoes this transition and new view of the world.

> As we move from an industrial to an information society, we will use our brainpower to create instead of our physical power, and the technology of the day will extend and enhance our mental ability (1982, 279–80).

Computer technology provides us the means instantly to access millions of facts and figures, thereby creating a potential information overload. This same technology forces us to change how we view information as the concern is no longer with its acquisition, but with its selection and application. Society's economic base has grown from the production of goods to the management and dissemination of information. Such changes are indicative of the shift from an industrial age to an information age.

The Industrial Society

The classic symbol of Industrial-Age thinking was the assembly line. The production of goods was seen to be most efficiently performed by breaking down the entire process into specific tasks. These tasks typically involved physical rather than mental work and were conceived as sequential. A worker was given one and only one task to perform over and over and did not directly see the finished product, but rather only his or her particular effort. The impact of any one individual was only in relation to those directly in line with him or her. The assembly line thus became the metaphor of a world conceived in mechanical terms, comprised of parts that functioned according to unchanging principles and laws.

The Information Society

The Information Age reflects ideas fundamentally opposite ideas from those of the Industrial Age as wholistic approaches are taken in attempting to understand a phenomena. Rather than breaking it down, one looks at it as part of a larger whole (Romberg 1984, 16). This perspective views the world not in terms of parts, but rather as relationships that interact in multi-dimensional ways. The simple linear, cause-and-effect model gives way to a more complex interactive model.

The multidimensional aspect of thinking in the Information Age is seen in the importance of networks and horizontal rather than vertical flow of communication, ideas, and power.

> This newly evolving world will require its own structures. We are beginning to abandon the hierarchies that worked well in the

centralized, industrial era. In their place, we are substituting the network model of organization and communication, which has its roots in the natural, egalitarian, and spontaneous formation of groups among like-minded people. Networks restructure the power and communication flow within an organization from vertical to horizontal (Naisbitt 1982, 281).

The impact of this can be characterized by the way that the assembly line has come to be replaced by the quality circle. The quality circle is a small group of individuals doing similar work who meet to discuss and solve work-related problems. This structure allows individuals from diverse areas to communicate directly and share in the solutions to problems. Each individual is able to perceive his or her efforts in relation to the total project while being aware of the responsibilities of others.

The assembly line structure of the Industrial Age ensured that the flow of information and productivity was in one direction and thus linear. In contrast, the network encourages communication and interaction at many levels at once. Thinking and problem solving is no longer simple a matter of cause and effect, but rather constant interaction and interdependence. Analytical approaches in and of themselves are not enough—the overload of information and greater complexity of the problems themselves require synthesis, holistic approaches, and global perspectives.

The School in The Information Society

Not only must we react to the impact of change itself, but also the rate of that change. It would appear that the existence of change is indeed the one thing that will not change for our society. Naisbitt (1982, 9) suggests that this increase in the rate of change is a major distinction between an industrial and an information society.

> The restructuring of American from an industrial to an information society will easily be as profound as the shift from an agricultural society to an industrial society. But there is one important difference. While the shift from an agricultural to an industrial society took only two decades. Change is occurring so rapidly that there is no time to react; instead we must anticipate the future.

The shift from an industrial society to an information society and the need to anticipate the future will require an appropriate shift in how we approach and solve problems since they are neither independent nor isolated. Instead, problems must now be considered as existing within a system of related or collected problems. Because of this, solutions are short-lived since the answer in any one situation interacts with others and hence the whole (Romberg 1984, 18–19).

How will education be different in an information society? In suggesting what the future might be like, Bruce Joyce (1971, 311) anticipated this need for a different perspective for thinking about education.

> ...the great dynamic challenge of the future is to develop, in addition to more highly efficient structures for education, entirely new modes of education designed to help people create new solutions to problems and to define problems that were not perceived before at all.

The need for "entirely new modes of education" is in response to problems and situations that have never before existed. Educators find themselves as "unconscious technological experts" due to the wide media attention given to technology and its application and presence in everyday life. The vocabulary of technology has crept into our conversation. We no longer meet and work together, we "interface." Typewriters have been replaced by word processors and the computer has received national attention to the point of having the distinction of being the first inanimate object ever to receive *Time* magazine's "Man of the Year" award, appearing on the 1982 front cover.

In schools, teachers are confronted with students who are fascinated with technology and are computer experts in every sense of the word. Computers and technology have become buzz words in education, with school districts committing vast financial and human resources toward developing computer literacy.

The use of technology in education has met with varying degrees of success and acceptance. Much of what has occurred in schools can be described as taking the resources of the Information Age and applying the principles from the Industrial Society. Content areas have been broken down to basic skills that have been targeted by education software developers. Drill and practice has been the primary instructional approach resulting in self-paced experiences that reinforce low-level cognitive skills such as recall. Simply using computers as electronic workbooks, while a viable instructional activity, is not enough. The problem is one of a "Humpty-Dumpty curriculum" that contains isolated and fragmented pieces of a larger whole. How do we put Humpty back together again?

The potential for technology in education, and especially *music* education, is powerful. Technology has presented educators with a dynamic new medium that is flexible and capable of diverse instructional styles across the musical curriculum. It is a medium of such strength that it requires the rethinking of teaching and learning.

Mass storage devices and electronic retrieval systems present new ways of organizing knowledge and structuring curricular content. New possibilities and models exist that offer a new resource for developing and fostering flexibility in teaching. Technology also affords new ways of reflecting differences in learning.

Early views of computer-assisted instruction embraced the "time to learn" issue since instructional activities were student-paced. The present state of software and hardware development is sufficiently sophisticated to enable a sensitivity to other styles of learning. For example, learning experiences can be qualitatively different in their degree of structure and perceptual mode. The same technology that can present a highly-structured tutorial can also offer open-ended simulations and experiences.

Technology creates unique learning environments that present new possibilities and solutions to unique and novel problems. "What if..." questions can be explored by empowering the learner with resources and abilities never before possible. Active and "hands-on" creativity can be a part of every child's musical experience through discovery and simulation experiences. Computer hardware and software can be used to record, edit, and perform pieces by providing an environment in which the student's only concern is one of composition and improvisation, rather than one of technical performance ability. Freedom and flexibility are provided since composing an original work is not limited to what the student can or cannot play on a keyboard instrument. This uniqueness is further highlighted by the possibility of total student control over basic parameters of music such as timbre and articulation.

Such a musical environment parallels the science lab, which was designed toward experimentation and discovery learning (learning by doing). The idea of a laboratory is really an environment for teaching and learning that accommodates individual differences and interests while at the same time providing a resource for group and class instruction.

Desk-top music publishing can now do for musicians what word processors have done for writers by enabling the creativity of the individual to be released from the mechanical constraints of the craft. The teaching of English and reading has undergone its own revolution due to the ability for young students to create camera ready publications, complete with graphics and sophisticated layouts.

While we are all familiar with computers, many music educators are not aware of technological resources that have direct application for music. These include: Synthesizers and keyboards, tone generators (poly-timbral electronic instruments that connect to keyboards or other controllers, drum machines,

MIDI (Musical Instrument Digital Interface) connections for keyboards and computers, sequencers (which record musical performances in files for playback and editing), and transcription software (which produce traditional notation from sequencer files).

Of all music behaviors, composition best embodies the essence of synthesis. The student who can create his or her own music can truly manipulate the various musical elements into an expressive whole. The idea behind musical synthesis is not so much the product but the process—an exciting musical process that all students should be given opportunities to experience.

Composition tends to be the most neglected aspect of the traditional music curriculum for a variety of reasons. Most teachers have not had much experience themselves with either composition or improvisation except in the jazz idiom. This, coupled with the impression that compositional activities are an individual endeavor, results in a lack of such creative activities in the school music program.

Technology-assisted creativity is a developmental process—the first attempts will lack musicality and expressiveness. As students begin to listen and respond to their music while it unfolds, interesting events can be held. How did they like the music (and why) and how could it be improved. The instant playback and editing capability of computers allow group involvement in the composition process by providing for the free manipulation of musical elements and thus experiences in a process of music synthesis.

The rapidly evolving nature of technology demands a constant awareness and revision of current practice to realize technology's potential as a learning and teaching resource. Instructional technology should be thoughtfully conceived, creatively employed, and carefully adapted to the particular styles of both teacher and learner.

It is interesting that one of the ways in which musical creativity can be fully fostered and explored is through the same technology that has created the need for a shift in our thinking. Technology becomes humanizing by providing opportunities for musical and hence aesthetic expression.

The world is changing. Problems exist that were unheard of a decade ago. As educators, we must use such change as the impetus for taking a new and fresh look at how and why we do what we do. The exciting challenge of the Information Age is to maintain a global perspective that allows for flexibility. Our own thinking will be challenged as we strive to challenge the thinking of our students.

References

Foreword

Marzano, R.J., R.S. Brandt, C.S. Hughes, B.F. Jones, B.Z. Presseisen, S.C. Rankin, and C. Suhor. 1988. *Dimensions of Thinking: A framework for curriculum and instruction.* Alexandria, VA: Association for Supervision and Curriculum Development.

Chapter 1

Dowling, W.J., and D.L. Harwood. 1986. *Music cognition.* Orlando, FL: Academic Press.

Howell, P., I. Cross and R. West. 1985. *Musical structure and cognition.* London: Academic Press.

Langer, S.K. 1948. *Philosophy in a new key.* New York: New American Library.

Mandler, G. 1985. *Cognitive psychology: An essay in cognitive science.* Hillsdale, NJ: Lawrence Erlbaum Associates.

Neisser, U. 1976. *Cognition and reality: Principles and implications of cognitive psychology.* New York: W. H. Freeman.

Schwartz, P., and J. Ogilvy. 1979. *The emergent paradigm: Changing patterns of thought and belief.* Menlo Park, CA: Values and Lifestyles Program.

Sloboda, J.A. 1985. *The musical mind: The cognitive psychology of music* Oxford: Clarendon Press.

Chapter 2

Barell, J., R. Liebmann, and I. Sigel. 1988. Fostering thoughtful self-direction in students. *Educational Leadership* (Association for Supervision and Curriculum Development) 45, no. 7.

Brown, A. 1978. Knowing when, where and how to remember: a problem of metacognition. In *Advances in instructional psychology,* ed. R. Glaser. Hillsdale, NJ: Erlbaum.

Costa, A. 1984. "Mediating the metacognitive." *Educational Leadership* (Association for Supervision and Curriculum Development) 42, no. 3.

1985. How can we recognize improved student thinking? In *Developing minds: A resource book for teaching thinking,* ed. A. Costa. Alexandria, VA: Association for Supervision and Curriculum Development.

Flavell, J. 1976. Metacognitive aspects of problem solving. In *The nature of intelligence,* ed. L. Resnick. Hillsdale, NJ: Erlbaum.

Holt, J. 1964. *How children fail.* New York: Pitman.

Pogonowski, L. 1985. Attitude assessment of upper elementary students in a process-oriented music curriculum. *Journal of Research in Music Education* 33, no. 4.

————. In progress. Musical patterns and variations from the compositional perspectives of ten-year-old children.

Presseisen, B. J. 1985. *Thinking skills throughout the K-12 curriculum: A conceptual design.* Philadelphia: Research for Better Schools.

Chapter 3

Abeles, H.F., C.R. Hoffer, and R.H. Klotman. 1984. *Foundations of music education* . New York: Schirmer Books.

References

Baron, J.B. 1987. Evaluating thinking skills in the classroom. In *Teaching thinking skills: Theory and practice,* eds. J. B. Baron and R. J. Sternberg. New York: W. 'H. Freeman.

Biggs, J.B. and K.F. Collis. 1982. *Evaluating the quality of learning: The SOLO taxonomy.* New York: Academic Press.

Bloom, B.S., M.D. Englehart, E.J. Furst, W.H. Hill and D.R. Krathwohl, eds. 1956. *Taxonomy of educational objectives—Handbook I: Cognitive domain.* New York: David McKay.

DeTurk, M.S. 1988a. Evaluating Musical concept learning with the SOLO taxonomy. In *The Proceedings of the 1988 Southeastern Music Education Symposium,* ed. J. A. Braswell, 162–71. Athens: Georgia Center for Continuing Education, University of Georgia.

———. 1988b. The relationship between experience in performing music class and critical thinking about music. Doctoral dissertation, University of Wisconsin-Madison. Eisner, E. W. 1964. *Think with me about creativity: 10 essays on creativity.* Danville, NY: F.A. Owen Publishing.

Ennis, R. H. 1962. A concept of critical thinking. *Harvard Educational Review,* 32, no. 1: 83-111.

——— 1987. A taxonomy of critical thinking dispositions and abilities. In *Teaching thinking skills: Theory and practice,* eds. J. B. Baron and R. J. Sternberg. New York: W. H. Freeman.

Ernst, K. D., and C. L. Gary. 1965. *Music in general education.* Washington, DC: Music Educators National Conference.

Hoffer, C. R. 1973. *Teaching music in the secondary schools.* 2nd ed. Belmont, CA: Wadsworth.

Hudgins, B. B. 1966. *Problem solving in the classroom.* New York. Macmillan.

Hudgins, B. B., and S. Edelman. 1986. Teaching critical thinking skills to fourth and fifth graders through teacher-led small group discussions. *Journal of Educational Research* 79: 333–42.

Kratus, J. 1988. Evaluating children's creative processes and products in music. In *The proceedings of the 1988 Southeastern Music Education Symposium,* ed. J. A. Braswell, 10-22. Athens: Georgia Center for Continuing Education, University of Georgia.

Leonhard C., and R. House. 1959.*Foundations and principles of music education.* 2nd ed. New York: McGraw-Hill.

National Assessment of Educational Progress. 1970. *Music objectives.* Ann Arbor, MI: National Assessment of Educational Progress.

Pogonowski, L. 1987. Developing skills in critical thinking and problem solving. *Music Educators Journal* 73, no. 6: 37–41.

Schwadron, A. A. 1967. *Aesthetics: Dimensions for music education.* Washington, DC: Music Educators National Conference.

Sidnell, R. 1973. *Building instructional programs in music education.* Englewood Cliffs, NJ: Prentice-Hall.

Thomas, Ronald B. 1970. Rethinking the curriculum. *Music Educators Journal* 56, no. 6: 68–70.

Chapter 4

Bennett, S. 1976. The process of musical creation: Interviews with eight composers. *Journal of Research in Music Education* 24, 3–14.

Flower, L. A., and Hayes, J. R. 1981. A cognitive process theory of writing. *College Composition and Communication* 32, 365–87.

Klausmeier, Herbert J. 1985. *Educational psychology* 5th ed. New York: Harper & Row.

Chapter 6

Beyer, B. K. 1987. *Practical strategies for the teaching of thinking.* Boston: Allyn and Bacon.

———. 1988. *Developing a thinking skills program.* Boston: Allyn and Bacon.

Stahl,. R. J. 1985. Cognitive information processes and processing within a uniprocess superstructure/microstructure framework: A practical information-based model. Unpublished manuscript, University of Arizona, Tuscon.

Chapter 7

Clark, B. 1986. *Optimizing learning: The integrative education model in the classroom.* Columbus. Merrill Publishing Co.

Frost, J.L. 1985. "Toward an integrated theory of play." in *The young child and music,* ed. J. Boswell, (1–24). Reston, VA: Music Educators National Conference.

Hohmann, M. B. Banet and D.P. Weikart. 1979. *Musical growth and development: Birth through six.* New York: Schirmer Books.

Chapter 8

Lipman, M. 1988. Critical thinking—what can it be? *Educational Leadership* 46, no. 1: 38–43.

Reahm, D. E. 1986. Developing critical thinking through rehearsal techniques. *Music Educators Journal* 72, no. 7: 29–31.

Small, A. R. 1987. Music teaching and critical thinking: What do we need to know? *Music Educators Journal* 74, no. 1: 46–49.

Chapter 9

Hodkinson, S. 1973. *A contemporary primer for band* (Volumes 1–3). Bryn Mawr, PA: Merion Music.

Olson, G. 1978. Developing student independence in identifying wind music for leisure activities. *Wisconsin School Musician* 47, no. 3: 7–12.

Chapter 11

DeLorenzo, L. C. 1987. Critical thinking: A Perspective for music educators. *Tempo,* 20–21.

Goodlad, J. I. 1983. What some schools and classrooms teach. *Educational Leadership* 40, no. 7.

Sternberg, R. J. 1987. Teaching critical thinking: Eight easy ways to fail before you begin. *Phi Delta Kappan,* 456-59.

Chapter 12

Joyce, B. 1971. The curriculum worker of the future. In *The Curriculum: Retrospect and Prospect.* Chicago, IL: National Society for the Study of Education, 70th yearbook, 307–55.

Naisbitt, J. 1982. *Megatrends.* New York: Warner Books.

References

Romberg, Thomas A. (1984). Curricular Reform in School Mathematics: Past Difficulties, Future Possibilities. Paper prepared for the Fifth International Congress on Mathematical Education (ICME 5). Adelaide, South Australia.

1081-2M-10-6/89